C000126186

River Days,

I always look forward to one of Mark Abramson's memoirs but with *River Days, River Nights*, he has notched up his game. The Russian River has been one of the most storied of U.S. gay resorts. In his usual modest, straightforward but always readable manner, Mark shows us what it was like for someone who lived and worked there year after year. He brings the unique local characters, visitors, venues, and entertainers to life, and also creates a vibrant cultural history.

> —Felice Picano, author of *Justify My Sins: A Hollywood Novel in Three Acts*

"As a longtime eyewitness of the Russian River, I found Mark's book wonderfully engaging and historically valuable."

> —Jack Fritscher, author of *Mapplethorpe: Assault with a Deadly Camera*.

"Mark Abramson has written another wonderful memoir; a poignant, sexy and sometimes hilarious reminiscence of a moment in time when gay men created a magical community on the banks of a river winding through a redwood forest.

> —Cleve Jones, author of *When We Rise: My Life in the Movement*

Mark's trademark hashtag is #ILOVEMYLIFE and it's not hard to see why when you read his remarkable multi-volume diaries. He processes his adventures as a gay man in San Francisco with self-effacing warmth and impressive attention to detail. His work is bound to conjure up your own memories of days gone by."

—Armistead Maupin, author of *Tales of the City* and *Logical Family: A Memoir*

"A sweet nostalgic romp into the woods of the Russian River, an enchanted Northern California gay resort. *River Days, River Nights* is Mark Abramson's valentine to the halcyon days of a bygone era (but not gone from the author's memory!). A time when waiters took acid, spinning mirror balls and free poppers fueled the tribal ritual on the dance floor, and Sylvester, Elvis Presley's love child, Betty Hutton, Edith Massey, Etta James, Eartha Kitt, Charles Pierce, Christine Jorgensen, Mr. Drummer and Divine covered the river front."

—Marc Huestis, author of *Impresario of Castro Street*

Mark's writing is superb and *River Days, River Nights* is no exception. Read it for a tender look back at a much more innocent time in gay life.

—Race Bannon, author, writer, and community organizer

"Step into Mark Abramson's time machine and be whisked away to the Golden Age of Gay! Once upon a time San Francisco was a party town, and when it came time for summer vacation, a good bit of that party relocated to the country. There, amidst the winding waters of the Russian River and majestic redwood forests, gay men (and a few women) reveled with hedonist abandon. Mark cleverly contrived to be in the very center of the revelry, and in his fast-paced memoir you'll read about sex, bars, parties, cabaret stars, disco divas, more sex, Divine, drugs, booze, leather, and even more sex. Anyone interested in what gay life was like between Stonewall and the plague years will surely want to read *River Days, River Nights*.

—Alvin Orloff, author of *Disasterama! - adventures in the queer underground 1977-1997*

"Hilarious, sexy, nostalgic, and a historically informative document of gay culture, *River Days, River Nights* is a welcome addition to author Mark Abramson's collection of endearing memoirs."

—Jim Provenzano, author of *PINS, Now I'm Here* and other novels

ALSO BY MARK ABRAMSON

Beach Reading,
a mystery series set in the Castro

Beach Reading
Cold Serial Murder
Russian River Rat
Snowman
Wedding Season
California Dreamers
Love Rules

Memoirs & Journals

For My Brothers
*Sex, Drugs & Disco – San Francisco Diaries
    from the Pre-AIDS Era*
*MORE Sex, Drugs & Disco – San Francisco
    Diaries from the Pre-AIDS Era*
Minnesota Boy
Farm Boy

River Days, River Nights

…true gay adventures at the Russian River

(1976 – 1984)

Mark Abramson

MINNESOTA BOY PRESS
SAN FRANCISCO CA

Copyright 2020 by Mark Abramson. All rights reserved. No part of this book may be reproduced or transmitted in any form or by any means, electronic or mechanical, including photocopying, recording, or by any information storage and retrieval system, without permission in writing from the publisher.

Published by Minnesota Boy Press

MinnesotaBoyPress@gmailcom

www.markabramson.net

ISBN-13: 9798613111299

Published April 1, 2020

Book Design: Toby Johnson

Thanks to the *Bay Area Reporter* for the cover photo, which appeared captioned "Gay by nature: river revelers relax in 1978," accompanying an article by Jack Fritscher, July 31, 2012, with Photo Credit: Morehead.

Special thanks to all of those who helped jog my memory about the amazing years I spent at the Russian River, including Steve Rickabaugh, Earl Rodier, Jim Knight, Gail Wilson, Sharon McNight, Sonny Cline, John Ponce, and Jim Provenzano, whose suggestion to check out the *Bay Area Reporter*'s on-line archives opened up a whole big world of long-forgotten memories.

I am extremely grateful to Michael Mayer, a man I have never met, who created an amazing web-site about the Hexagon House/Woods resort. I have tried time and again but failed to reach out to thank him and his husband, Carl Bruno, who was one of the three owners of The Woods. http://www.thewoods-hexagonhouse.com

Great thanks go to Gary Brownen and Nile Eckhoff for tons of technical assistance and moral support, from proofreading to photoshopping and most of all to Toby Johnson who knows how to put my jumbled life together in book form. I wouldn't have known where to begin and I am blessed to know you all!

For a nostalgic look back at the gay nude beach near Wohler Bridge, check out this short film thanks to Jack Fritscher: *Cruising Elsewhere* by Ryan White
https://vimeo.com/344887359

Mark Abramson
San Francisco, California
February 14, 2020

Wohler Bridge

Contents

CHAPTER ONE:
Wohler Beach

The first time I saw the Russian River must have been the summer of 1976. I moved from Minneapolis to San Francisco in 1975 and Armando, my first serious boyfriend, took me there. He had grown up in Los Angeles and California was all new to me, so he introduced me to a lot of things, from real Mexican food to Quaaludes to nude beaches. We mostly took day trips, across the Golden Gate Bridge, through the rainbow tunnel and then an hour north on Highway 101 through Marin and Sonoma Counties. Just north of Santa Rosa is the turn-off to the Russian River.

We drove west on River Road through orchards and vineyards to the turn-off for Wohler Bridge. Everyone parked their cars there and walked the rest of the way through a big open field. Armando told me the land belonged to the actor Fred McMurray, best known as the father in the old TV show "My Three Sons" that most of us had grown up watching. We must have figured that Mr. McMurray was too busy in Hollywood to care that hundreds of gay men were traipsing through his property all summer long.

We walked about a mile through tall grasses to reach our destination. So many years have passed that it's hard to judge spatial distance from such a great distance in time, but eventually we entered trees and scrub brush on narrow paths that led to the secluded gay nude beach on the Russian River. It was paradise.

Having grown up in Minnesota, the "land of lakes," I always loved being near water, but while living in San Francisco I spent most of my days off from work riding the #38 Geary bus to the end of the line and walking down to the gay nude beach at Land's End, lying out in the sun on the sand between huge boulders, listening to the crashing waves of the Pacific and watching the parade of naked young men walk by.

The Russian River was serene compared to Land's End. The water flowed slowly and we, just as slowly, unwound from our lives in the city as we passed joints back and forth, drank beer we'd brought in our Styrofoam coolers and ate the sandwiches we had made at home that morning. Sometimes we walked beyond the nude beach and met other naked guys on the paths through the forest.

There were no gay businesses in Guerneville yet. Armando had taken me to breakfast once at the River Inn, that classic American diner next to the gas station on the east end of Main Street. We had Swedish pancakes and grilled ham steaks with the bone in the middle and looked out the big windows at tourists pulling campers with canoes and fishing poles strapped on top, but I had already discovered Armando had a mean jealous streak. I remember that morning's great food being ruined by a huge fight when he decided that someone in a booth across the way was checking me out when I went to the restroom, which he insisted was my fault. "Enough!" I said.

There were too many beautiful men in my world to be saddled with a jealous lover. Thousands more were arriving in San Francisco every week, filling the streets and bars in the Polk Gulch, Tenderloin and South of Market. There was a gay bar in nearly every neighborhood of the city, from Nob Hill to Dick's at the Beach. The Haight had nearly a dozen and the Castro was just starting to come alive. Many of the bars opened at 6 a.m. and they filled up at 6 a.m. too.

During those few years after I moved out of Armando's place on Grove Street, the latter part of the seventies in San Francisco, I was on sexual overdrive, making up for lost time. There were about a dozen bathhouses open 24/7. The bars south of Market all had dark back rooms where guys could get it on. There were sex-clubs too, places with names like the Glory Holes, the Corn Holes, and the Boot Camp, which was mostly for guys into water sports, and the Sling, or did that come a little later? The Castro had the Jaguar book store, where no one ever went to browse, at least not for books.

I had a few relationships too, during those post-Armando years, of various degrees of depth and longevity. Most of those boyfriends became real friends when the initial intensity wore off, some remaining friends with occasional benefits. At the very least they all became the sort of people with whom I would share a hug when I ran into them afterwards. Even Armando and I became like family, eventually.

I enjoyed the Russian River a lot more after Armando and I split up and I started going to Wohler Beach with friends. I had too many men to choose from or to choose just *one* from, and here they all were, lying out naked among the redwoods, cruising the vineyards and forests along the sparkling blue waters of the river.

After sunbathing, swimming, and sometimes sex in the bushes, my friends and I always stopped at the Rusty Nail. It was the only local gay bar in those days, right on River Road on our way back toward the freeway. The Rusty Nail had a big parking lot and a patio where they barbecued on weekends. This was the time of day when we ran into everyone we'd seen at the beach earlier, but now we got to see them up close and wearing just enough clothes to leave something to the imagination.

We might have a second beer at the Rusty Nail, shoot a game of pool or two, and meet new people, make plans to get together in the city, and exchange phone numbers. In those days, we had rotary phones with cords on them, oftentimes only one phone for a whole flat full of roommates, where someone would answer and the others would yell some variation of: "If it's my mother, I'm too stoned to talk. Tell her I'm not home!"

CHAPTER TWO:
The Lodge and Michael Greer

It was a summer or two later when we discovered the next gay attraction up north, the Russian River Lodge, just down the road from the Rusty Nail. A couple named Sam and Jim owned the place and rented out rooms upstairs in the main house and a row of cabins along the driveway. Sam and Jim had an open relationship, so I had sex with both of them a few times, individually and together in a threesome. There was no jealousy there and I thought this was more like what I needed in my life in my twenties.

The Russian River Lodge had a tree-house big enough for four or five guys and a shed on the hillside with slings and glory holes. It had a huge clothing-optional swimming pool and a campground. If the rooms were full we would camp out on the thick grass. Those were my first overnight stays at the river. We didn't have a tent, just sleeping bags and pillows from home.

I remember the first time I woke up with a ten-inch yellow banana slug on my pillow, staring me in the eye. When I mentioned it to someone at the lodge later that day, they told me the locals held a Slug Festival every year including banana slug races and a bake-off in which slugs were made into such gastronomic delights as slug Wellington, slug enchiladas and slug sushi. Vegetarianism sounded suddenly appealing.

My best buddy Bill and I were lunchtime waiters at the Bank Exchange restaurant in the Transamerica Pyramid building and we also worked weekends at a place called *Up & Coming* on 18ᵀᴴ Street in the Castro. We usually had Mondays off so we often drove up to the River after our Sunday dinner shift. We tried to make it to the Rusty Nail in time for last call and then head over to the Russian River Lodge, which was usually jumping after the bar closed. Men were all over that hillside, the tree house hosting a moonlit orgy with dozens more guys in and around the shed. Sometimes they built a big bonfire near the campground where we could take a break from cruising. Men would be standing around the flames or sitting on logs, talking softly by the crackling fire amid sounds of cigarette lighters snapping shut, belts unbuckled, slurping, moans, and gasps whenever someone came.

One week Bill and I got a Tuesday off too, so we stayed an extra night at the Lodge. They told us that Monday nights were "locals' night" with live entertainment at a place called The Woods, two miles north of Guerneville near the entrance to Armstrong Redwoods State Park. The Woods was trying to become a gay bar in a big modern room annexed onto a beautiful old stone and wooden building called The Hexagon House. The place had been bought by three gay guys from Los Angeles.

Bill and I were late and the show had already started but the host made room for us at a table right inside the door. I remember a fan blowing on us full blast because it was so hot that night. The entertainer was a tall guy with a deep voice and a handsome rubbery face. He told stories and sang sad songs and some comic ones. His name was Michael Greer and I would get to know him well over the next couple of decades

Michael Greer was best known for the movies The Gay
Deceivers and Fortune in Men's Eyes, but he also played the emcee in
Better Midler's first film, The Rose. Michael Greer's impersonation
of Bette Davis was so perfect that they hired him to dub some of
her lines in the TV miniseries The Dark Secret of Harvest Home
in 1978 and again, a few years after I met him, in Bette Davis' last
film, Wicked Stepmother in 1989.

Michael Greer

I had already seen Michael Greer in movies, but I didn't realize who he was that night at The Woods. Bill and I were amused by some of his jokes, but we had smoked a lot of pot before the show and were too stoned to fully appreciate his act. We were probably horny too and wanted to go check out the Rusty Nail before we headed back to the Lodge.

I never saw the Hexagon House restaurant in full swing and I only peeked in there that night when the room was dark. I would hear enough about it over the next few years that I could picture it with candlelit tables, Lalique crystal vases displayed in glass cases that lined the elegant six-sided dining room. The building was nearly three stories high with six enormous Douglas fir logs at the corners of the main room meeting like a teepee above the roof. A huge stone fireplace stood on one side and there was a smaller lounge and piano bar off to the north. This fabulous building was the centerpiece of a five-acre resort with Fife Creek running through the middle of it.

HEXAGON HOUSE

Gourmet Dining
featuring
Continental Cuisine

invites you to meet
Betty Hutton

•Garden Resort
•Motor Lodge
•Cabanas
•Fine Antique Collection

Miss Hutton will be with us through July. During the evening have Miss Hutton autograph your menu.

Dinner Thursday-Monday 6 to 10
Sunday Champagne Brunch 10-2

Live Entertainment in our Beautiful Lounge

Call for Reservations

HEXAGON HOUSE   707-869-3991

16881 Armstrong Woods Rd., Guerneville

I read that the main building had been created to be used as an art school back in the 1940s, but it had been a fine-dining restaurant for years. The three gay owners were old friends of the movie musical star Betty Hutton, who would come up from Hollywood for long stays in the summer. Sometimes she greeted dinner patrons at the door and acted as an unofficial hostess. After dinner she might even sing a few numbers at the piano lounge on the north side of the restaurant, a special treat for her old fans.

I heard that one of the tabloids wrote an article saying that Betty Hutton's career had so totally collapsed that she was now reduced to working as a waitress in a coffee shop in the middle of nowhere in northern California where she hoped no one would recognize her in her utter embarrassment. Fake news was thriving, even then.

Betty Hutton never performed at The Woods after it was no longer the elegant Hexagon House restaurant. She came around, though. I remember her showing up one hot summer afternoon at one of the bars. Even though she was wearing huge dark sunglasses, I heard one of the bartenders yell, "Betty Hutton! Girl...I knew that was you behind those Foster Grants! How the hell are ya'?"

One summer Betty had a wealthy "gentleman friend" who wanted to rent the entire resort for a couple of weeks for just the two of them without anyone else around. I'm not sure if he was being romantic or homophobic or both, but it was the peak of the season and there was no way the owners would put the whole staff out of work for two weeks and besides, many of the rooms and cabins were already reserved months ago by people from all over the world. That summer was the last time I saw Betty Hutton, who died many years later at age 86 in 2007.

CHAPTER THREE:
"Go west, young men, go west!"

During those few years since I first went to the beach near Wohler Bridge, gays were opening new businesses in Guerneville and all around it. Guerneville had been a resort town since the late nineteenth century, when well-off San Franciscans rode a ferry across the bay to the narrow gauge railway train to resorts or summer homes all along the river. By the '50s, more people were coming by car than by train, and for a time it was quite a biker town. There was massive flooding in the '60s, followed by an influx of flower children. Someone told me when I first moved up north that the resort community thrived whenever the economy was bad. When it was good, people could afford to travel further away, to Hawaii or Mexico or even Europe. Another reason for the gay expansion was that in 1976 California repealed its anti-sodomy laws. Until then it had been illegal to simply *be* gay, much less advertise that you were running an establishment that catered to gays.

In 1978, a gay man named Peter Pender, who was a nationally well-known champion of the card game Bridge, moved west from Philadelphia and bought an old resort called Murphy's. He renamed it Fife's for Fife Creek, which ran through the property and it became the town's first gay resort. The sexual revolution was going on across the country, especially in San Francisco, so it was only logical that it would spread to the nearest resort area.

Fife's was just west of Guerneville, with a bar and restaurant, a swimming pool surrounded by little cabins, and a campground right on the Russian River. A few years later when The Woods opened two miles north of town and was drawing thousands of gays to dance every weekend, Peter Pender opened a discotheque across the road from Fife's and named it Drums. It too had a swimming pool beside it, with state-of-the-art sound and lights and a DJ for the dance floor.

I had stayed at Fife's once on a long weekend "honeymoon" with my old boyfriend Kap. It was nice, but a little too tasteful for me, comparable to a Polk Gulch bar at the time. I had always felt more comfortable in the Castro or South of Market than on Polk Street. Fife's campground was usually cruisy at night, but it was even better known for some of the gay campers who pitched their tents there. They would celebrate birthdays and special events by covering the picnic tables in linen tablecloths and set them with the finest silverware and china someone had inherited from his grandmother. It wasn't unusual to see elaborate floral arrangements and huge antique candelabras. Those queens would serve Russian caviar and grilled salmon, fresh sautéed green beans with almonds, expensive champagne and for dessert, they'd somehow whip up a Grand Marnier soufflé with only a camping stove.

I exaggerate, of course, but they did go all out. In one of the books in my Beach Reading mystery series, a group of friends haul a baby grand piano to the campground at Fife's where they have a hired pianist play classical music in the nude while they dine al fresco. These days, sadly, the former Fife's resort is a popular setting for heterosexual weddings.

⤬

Back in San Francisco, there was a bar on the corner of Duboce and Valencia Streets called the Rainbow Cattle Company. It attracted a mixed crowd of cowboy types and bikers and quite a few hippies thrown into the mix. I didn't go there often, even when I lived in SOMA, but it was an okay place. The bar is called Zeitgeist now, a German bier garden with food and it's hardly gay at all.

When it was still the Rainbow Cattle Company, I spent a night with a guy I met at the bar who lived upstairs, so I told everyone at work the next day that I had spent the night "over the rainbow." I thought I had made up a funny new catch-phrase, but it turned out other people had been saying it for years. Several of the guys who lived upstairs were known for picking up strangers at the bar and inviting them to their rooms.

Those rooms "over the rainbow" were nothing fancy, just a bed, a desk, and a sink. Toilets and showers were down the hall. Some guys built lofts for their beds to create more floor room and brought in a hot plate and mini-fridge, sealed food containers to discourage the cockroaches, TV sets and stereos and some of them even had slings, I heard. Everyone was a "friend of Judy" up there.

When it was still a gay bar, the owner decided to clone a copy of the Rainbow Cattle Company right in the middle of the main street of the sleepy little town of Guerneville and "Whoo-yeah!" a shit-kicking country gay bar was born! The RBCC at the Russian River was only one story tall, so there were no rooms upstairs. It had a couple of pool tables and a big bar in the center of the room with access from all sides. It was the place to go to watch the Russian River Rodeo parade every summer. A gang of gay guys always hung out in front of the Rainbow to see the little girls with tassels on their tall white boots trying to side-step piles of manure from the horses that led the parade, but one of them would always drop her baton in it anyway.

I'm not sure whether the Stumptown (Guerneville's nickname because of all of the trees that were cut down to make room for the town) Parade is still connected to the Russian River Rodeo or not, but the Rainbow Cattle Company is still a thriving gay bar to this day and I hope it lasts forever.

Just past Fifes (and Drums) was Fern Grove, a quiet little place owned by a semi-retired gay couple. It had no bar, no restaurant, no dance floor, but it had a lovely pool and cozy knotty-pine cottages and was within easy walking distance of town.

Farther west of town was Molly Brown's, named for the Unsinkable Mollie Brown, played by Debbie Reynolds in the movie, who survived the sinking of the Titanic. Molly Brown's was a bar with a restaurant attached. I liked the food there and part of it was a place where you could eat outdoors. It was directly in the flood plain and even though the building was up on stilts, there was a sign on one wall that pointed to the level of the stain from the last flood. It was taller than I am and I think I remember seeing their waterlogged piano sitting there too. The place was far from unsinkable and I can only imagine that they got tired of going through all that clean-up every time the river left its banks.

On the opposite side of River Road from Molly Brown's was a gay dance hall called Silverado. I went there once or twice because I was always working during its busy times. It was later renamed the Mine Shaft and the Bayou, if I'm not mistaken.

The straight resort called Highland Park became the gay resort Highlands when Steve Rickabaugh and Bill Haugan bought it with a short-term third partner, John Shambre. It had cabins, a hot-tub, and a beautiful swimming pool on a hillside just above the Guerneville library on the east edge of town. They had a pool table in the main house and the pool and hot tub were clothing-optional.

River Village Resort was just east out of town on River Road, on the side away from the river and usually above the flooding. They had cabins around a pristine swimming pool, well landscaped with colorful splashes of flowers in bloom and a wonderful restaurant with a small bar attached. I loved going there for dinner because it was almost fine dining, but a bit countrified. It was a gay resort, so I guess you would say it was a gay bar, but it wasn't one that a person would go to unless they were having dinner or staying there.

The Willows was east of Guerneville too, but on the river side of the road. It was more of a guest house and I think they allowed camping. There was no bar or restaurant, but the place was very lush and green with a wide expanse of lawn and willow trees and a row of canoes for rent. The only time I can ever remember going there was one Saturday afternoon. I met two stunning young guys from Seattle, a couple who were on vacation and persuaded me to come back with them to the Willows where they were staying for a three-way. It was a first for me—not my first threesome, but my first time at an unusual sexual position. They were both amazing and so hot that I will never forget them.

One block off Guerneville's main drag at the corner of Fourth and Mill Streets was an old resort called Hetzel's. Two gay guys named Marvin and Rudy bought the place around 1980 and changed the name to the Russian River Resort or the Triple-R, which is still thriving under the name R-3 Resort all these years later. It has rooms with wood-burning stoves, so it's open year-round unless it's closed due to flooding. There's a full bar and a decent restaurant and a nice-sized pool with lots of room to sunbathe around it.

CHAPTER FOUR:
The blue house on Orchard Avenue

Jonathan was probably the richest of all my ex-boyfriends in San Francisco. In the fall of 1980 he bought a house at the river and decided that his friends would help him fix it up in exchange for having a place to stay for free on their days off. His two roommates and best friends in the city, Bobby and Bob, also ran their own businesses. Bobby laid carpets and linoleum for a living and Bob installed and refinished hardwood floors. Both of them owned a lot of tools and were pretty good carpenters too. I wasn't nearly as good at anything relevant to the remodeling job, but I could handle a paint brush and I could cook.

Most evenings we ate out, though. There are dozens of wonderful restaurants all over the wine country. We would drive over to Occidental for dinner at Negri's or the Union Hotel, both family-style Italian restaurants at the center of that tiny town. They served all-you-can-eat, course after course of delicious Minestrone soup and bread and salad and bread and pasta and still more bread and finally the main course. I knew I would be too full by then, so I usually tried to order something I could take home for a midnight snack or for lunch the next day. They had great friend chicken, which doesn't sound especially Italian, but it was delicious cold.

During that winter of remodeling, Bob and Bobby and Jon and I usually ended up at the Rusty Nail. That was where I first met one of the most stunning young men I had ever seen, named John Ponce. I was in my late twenties and he was a little younger than me, but he already owned his own home in Monte Rio, right next to the entrance to the Bohemian Grove (more on that later) and was dabbling in other real estate in Sonoma County.

John Ponce was over six feet tall with olive skin, black hair, perfect white teeth, and a "body to die for." There weren't any gyms at the River yet—gyms were just starting to cater to gay men in the city—but John had his own gym at his house and it showed. He rarely wore a shirt inside the bar, so I could watch the smooth muscles of his back and shoulders as he leaned over the pool table to make his shot. John was the only guy I knew on the River who had his own personal sling and he also happened to be hung like a horse!

My friend Jonathan's house was on Vacation Beach on the south side of the Russian River about two miles past the old Guerneville Bridge. The main house was on two levels. The downstairs living room had sliding glass doors leading directly onto an indoor swimming pool. The first thing we did was rip the roof off that pool. We wanted sunshine, ruddy cheeks and tan lines. We were much too gay to swim indoors!

By spring of that year, Jon had turned the garage and the top floor of the house into two nice studio apartments with track lighting and the latest in modern appliances. Over the course of that winter I realized that I needed a break from city life in San Francisco and decided to move up to the river full-time. I paid $375/month for the main part of the house, which was a lot of money at the time, especially since Jonathan had been using it every weekend that winter during the remodel. Once I started paying rent, he had a hard time adjusting to the fact that the place was "mine" now.

Mark on the day we tore the roof off the pool

Jonathan finally decided to take the studio apartment we built in the old garage to use on weekends. He built a big redwood deck onto it, twice the size of the studio, overlooking a flower and vegetable garden that we planted that spring. Bobby rented the upstairs studio for the first year or so and when Bob came up he pitched a tent in the side yard.

My next step was to find a job. I had worked as a waiter since I arrived in San Francisco in 1975. I had also done a lot of bartending at the sort of private events where they wanted a young man in tight black pants with crisp white shirtsleeves rolled up to expose his forearms. I had gotten to know a few people at the River besides Sam and Jim at the Lodge and the gorgeous John Ponce. I asked around and applied at a couple of places and the next thing I knew I was offered a waiter job at The Woods, the place Bill and I had gone to see Michael Greer. I don't think they cared as much about my resume as the fact that I already had a place to live. Hiring seasonal help is tricky for that reason.

During the winter while we were remodeling Jon's house the owners of The Woods turned the old Hexagon House restaurant into a beautiful dance floor with inlaid wood, a disc jockey booth on one side and an impressive set of lights and special effects machines overhead. I got to know a waitress and a couple of waiters—all locals—who had been doing fine dining service there for the past few seasons. Now that the main room had been turned into a dance floor, the annex—where I had seen Michael Greer perform—became the dining room, with the same style of service as the old place, at least at first. That meant offering chilled forks with the salad course and warmed spoons for the soup. I had been a waiter at Mama's on Nob Hill and served dozens of celebrities, but I had never heard of such a thing as freezing forks and warming soup spoons.

CHAPTER FIVE:
Floods

I moved into the main part of Jonathan's house on Orchard Avenue in late winter, before the tourist season started. It was one of the many years when the Russian River flooded its banks. I was having a beer at the bar at Fife's one afternoon when someone ran inside and announced that the parking lot would be underwater soon, so we should all move our cars up onto the road. The bar and restaurant were up a flight of stairs, so they were probably going to be fine, but the parking lot and most of the cabins would flood that night.

Somehow, I got involved with a group of guys helping to do pre-flood damage control. First we went to each of Fife's cabins, placed the television on top of the bed and hoisted the bed up in the air to suspend it from hooks on the ceiling. Here I'd always thought those hooks were for hanging slings! There must have been at least six of us, all guys in our twenties, healthy and strong. When we finished at Fife's we set out in the pouring rain—night had fallen by this time—to do more good deeds along the road leading out of town. I don't know who organized this endeavor, but I remember hauling a heavy chest freezer up from the basement of one elderly couple and lots of furniture moving at other homes. People were extremely grateful. We finally all ended up at the Rainbow Cattle Company until last call and I thought it would have been nice if someone had bought us a round to thank us for all the hard work.

We were just a bunch of guys doing what we could to help, doing what needed to be done, doing what we were told, like good Christian Boy Scouts, the way most of us had been raised, not really expecting anything in return. It should have come as no surprise a few years later when AIDS came along that we worked so hard helping our friends while they fought for their lives.

Neeley Road was underwater that night, so I couldn't get home, but someone offered me a dry place to spend the night until the floodwaters went back down. I would see worse floods over the following seasons, but that was my first. The Russian River flooded its banks to some extent almost every winter that I lived there.

At Jon's house the swimming pool overflowed during heavy rains and water would seep in through the walls around the sliding glass doors into the lower level of the living room. I often went out there in the morning to discover big ugly potato bugs in the bottom of the swimming pool and mushrooms growing out of the brand new carpet. Bobby thought they might be fun to eat, but I disagreed. I've tried all sorts of mushrooms including psilocybin ones, but these were the exact same color blue as the carpet. I figured they must be filled with whatever chemicals were in the blue dye. They might have given us a trip alright, but more likely a trip to the emergency room.

We usually got a warning from the radio or TV news about what time the river would crest and how high. The house on Orchard Avenue was high enough that I never felt unsafe, even when the blue mushrooms were growing in the living room. The rest of my apartment was up three or four steps from the pool level and even if the water came up that high I could use the apartment on the top floor. Bobby rarely came up on weekdays during the rainy season and I had a set of keys. My only real problem was when Neeley Road flooded. It was my only way out of Vacation Beach without a boat. I always gave myself plenty to time to drive into Guerneville, have a few beers at the Rainbow Cattle Company, and find someone I hadn't already slept with (or who wanted a repeat) who lived on high ground or someone who was willing to come over and get flooded in at my place for a day or two.

We would head over to Safeway and stock up on food that was easy to prepare and eat in the dark if the power went out. I had a flashlight and a gas stove, but still. We mostly stocked up on booze and ice… and grass! I fondly remember some erotic flooded honeymoons at the river.

My other option when the river flooded was to drive into San Francisco. I had plenty of friends with a guest room or a couch where I could sleep. I would usually spend those afternoons in the Castro—shopping, eating, and cruising—where all the bars were always jumping. Bear Hollow (at 440 Castro,) Toad Hall, Castro Station, the Elephant Walk, Midnight Sun, Twin Peaks, and Nothing Special were all on Castro Street. On 18TH Street I could choose between the Men's Room, the newly opened Moby Dick, the Village, the Pendulum, and the Eureka Valley Club, where the Edge stands now, and was the last straight bar in the neighborhood, just starting to welcome the new gay neighbors and their business.

Nights I would usually head South of Market. My friend Terry Thompson managed the Arena on 9TH and Harrison. He was like a big brother to me. The Stud was still on Folsom Street across from Hamburger Mary's and Cissy's Saloon. Febe's was going strong on 11TH and Folsom, but those guys seemed like serious bikers, a little too serious (and too old) for me. So did the men at the No-Name, now that I no longer had John Preston to keep me under his wing. He had moved on to write "Mister Benson" and live in L.A. by then or back to New York and wherever else in the world his wealthy clients bought him a plane ticket and paid all his expenses.

It wasn't that I didn't like older guys. I just didn't want to be seriously injured or killed in any rough sex games. There had been murders in the news lately too, guys who'd been picked up in leather bars south of Market. The older men who looked the scariest to me were probably more apt to take me home, feed me a hearty homemade meal, tuck me into bed and knit me a warm scarf and stocking cap for Christmas, but I couldn't be sure.

The Ambush was more to my taste. They didn't have a full liquor license, just beer and wine, but the place was always full of hot guys who worked blue-collar jobs, sexy regular guys, most of whom had moved to San Francisco in their twenties, just like I did.

I made even more friends in the city during those rainy California winters when I lived up north. I let them know they always had a place to crash when they came up to the Russian River, especially if they were fun people and/or great sex and/or had good drugs, especially cocaine.

CHAPTER SIX:
Carl, Gene & Al

My new bosses, the three owners of the Hexagon House, now The Woods Resort, were Carl Bruno, Gene Arnaiz and Al Knopka. Carl and Gene had been lovers back in L.A. before all three of them moved up to the river. Gene had a 98-year-old great aunt Maria Cordova, who had been a movie star in the age of silent films. She was a tiny woman who lived in an apartment upstairs from the old Hexagon House restaurant before the place went gay and they moved her to an old folks' home in Santa Rosa. I only saw her two or three times, always on Gene's arm. I remember watching the two of them trying to cross a threshold from one room into another. It was so low that the average person wouldn't even notice it, but she was so old and frail that she could only shuffle her feet. Gene simply picked her up and set her down again a few inches forward as if the two of them had practiced that little ballroom dance step a thousand times.

Al was the owner I got to know first. Before I started working Monday "locals' night," I always sat with Al at his table to watch the cabaret shows with two or three other guys about my age. He and Carl liked them young. Gene was only about a week older then me and I was only 28 when I started there.

Al would order Dom Perignon for our table, bottle after bottle, and since he was one of the owners, he never paid for it. It didn't take me long to realize that expensive champagne was wasted on my taste buds. About the only time I had ever drunk champagne was on New Year's Eve in a bar where they poured rot-gut cheap stuff for everyone to have a toast at midnight. Thinking back, I wonder if Al even tipped those poor cocktail waiters. If so, I doubt it was enough for putting up with our table of boisterous drunks, emptying our ashtrays of cigarette butts and tolerating Al's grab-ass routine.

It's funny how you can get to know someone by watching their behavior even more than by what they say. Al's grandiosity was balanced out by his cheapness, but it took me a while to discover that facet of his personality.

Al had an old white convertible and sometimes he let me drive it down to the city with him riding in the passenger's seat. One day we started out by stopping for gas in Guerneville. The tank was practically running on fumes and the oil stick was seriously low too. I said, "Al, you need at least a quart of oil. You wanna get it here, before we head to the freeway?"

"Nah," he said. "I know a cheaper place to buy it when we get to the city."

I was surprised we weren't smoking by the time we hit the Golden Gate Bridge, but such was Al's temperament. At some point during my time at The Woods, Al hooked up with a young boyfriend I want to call Carlos, although I'm not sure of his name. He was smoking hot and he knew it, but he was also as charmless to the rest of us as a Polk Street hustler who had fallen into a sweet gig. Carlos didn't like any of Al's friends and he let us all know that he was the center of Al's life now. And Al was so blindly in love or lust that he let Carlos do it.

It wouldn't have surprised me if Carlos had a few other "Als" in his life. He sometimes disappeared for weeks at a time, during which Al was good for nothing until Carlos returned. I couldn't trust that sexy jerk for as far as I could throw him.

CHAPTER SEVEN:
Cow shit and Clara

My first spring at the river, we put in a big flower and vegetable garden south of the house on Orchard Avenue. Either Bobby or Jon rented a roto-tiller to dig up the old weedy dirt and break up the clumps. We all spent a couple of weekends working on it and having grown up on a farm, I suggested that what it really needed was some good fertilizer.

One of the waiters I would soon be working with as soon at The Woods opened for the season was a guy I'll call David. He and his cowboy husband lived on a little acreage north of the coastal town of Bodega Bay, which was famous as the site of Alfred Hitchcock's classic *The Birds*. They only had one horse and a few head of cattle but they called it a ranch. What it did have was plenty of cow manure and they said I was welcome to "Come and get it!" in the words of Ma Kettle, played by the late, great Marjorie Main.

So I drove my pickup truck over to their ranch one Monday afternoon and David and I spent an hour or so shoveling shit into the back of my truck. We had lined the bed with black plastic garbage cans, but still it took until mid-summer before the smell faded away. Such was life in the country.

Once we got the truck filled to the brim we looked down and noticed that all four tires on my truck had gone flat from the weight of the cow manure. I wasn't about to undo all our work, so I drove on four flat tires very slowly and carefully, maybe three miles to the nearest gas station, just down the coast. I filled the tires and drove back to Guerneville, afraid all the way that they were going to pop.

I backed up to the garden, let down the tailgate and managed, all by myself, to shovel and sweep and push all that crap out of there. Yes, I was once a farm boy, but now I remembered one of the reasons I hadn't stayed on the farm. There was always too damn much hard work! I was done! The other guys could rent another roto-tiller on the weekend when they came up and they could deal with mixing all that rich ripe fertilizer into the soil.

Just when I finished emptying the truck, I noticed a little old lady coming out of the house that faced mine across the street. I can't remember her name, so I'll call her Clara, even though she must have died of old age years ago and couldn't sue me anyway. "Young man!" I heard her yelling at me from the middle of Orchard Avenue. She came right over to me and introduced herself. "Would you mind terribly helping me with something? I need to change a light bulb. I can't reach it without climbing up on something and I'm so afraid of falling and breaking a hip or…"

"Sure, I can do that. I'm just finishing up here."

The interior of her house was a perfect "little old lady" movie set, complete with rocking chair, framed photographs of family members on the walls above a dusty mantle over the fireplace and crocheted doilies everywhere. The light bulb that needed replacing was on the ceiling of the little pantry off the kitchen. I barely needed a footstool to replace it, but she was quite short.

"Thank you so much, young man. What did you say your name was?"

"I don't think I told you my name. It's Mark"

"Well, thank you so much, Mark. You can call me Clara."

"You're welcome, Clara. Any time."

But I didn't really mean *any* time! She started coming over every time she saw my truck pull in the driveway. "Mark, could you be so kind as to…bring in some more firewood? …help me shake out this old throw rug? …turn this potted plant so that it gets more sun? …move the tree limb that fell on the stairs out back?"

That was when I got to see the back of the house. It had once been beautifully terraced all the way down to the river, but now it was a jungle of weeds and brambles. I could barely see the steep stone stairway that zig-zagged down to the beach. The place would have been terrific if it were cleaned up. Let's see…riverside property in 1981? Jonathan bought his house across the street on Orchard Avenue for $80,000 and sold it when he started getting sick a few years later, for $125,000. Even without the swimming pool, hers would have been as valuable because it was right on the river.

I fantasized about getting together a few friends and some good tools out there on a nice day and cleaning up that whole hillside for her, but then I stopped myself. No, I didn't! What was I thinking? She had been taking advantage of my good nature for days. She was getting free labor, without ever offering to pay me with even a slice of pie or a piece of cake. She had never offered me so much as a glass of water. She wasn't even saying "thank you" any more. She was just getting to be annoying. Her voice hurt my ears and her helplessness was starting to feel like an act that I was tired of observing.

Jonathan, Bob, and Bobby all came up on the weekend, so there were three more vehicles in the driveway or on the street out front. I forgot all about the neighbor-lady Clara until sometime on Sunday afternoon. The guys had just finished mixing the cow manure into the garden soil and it was warm enough for us to lie out by the pool for a couple of hours before people started heading back to the city. The water in the pool wouldn't be warm enough to relax in it for a few more weeks, but Bobby probably dived in anyway. Something reminded me of Clara and I told the guys what had been going on with her daily chores for me.

"Oh, *no*, not Clara!" Bob yelled.

"You fell for her too?" Jon asked me. "I'm sorry. We should have warned you."

As it turned out, each of them had had their own encounters with Clara. They each told similar stories about how they had at first started doing simple chores for the sweet little old lady across the street, but also how she had become overbearing in her neediness, more and more demanding and much less grateful. I don't remember how my friends broke away from the habit of helping her. I don't remember how I did either. Maybe she died or maybe she knew that now that we were all together we would talk about her and the jig would be up.

Thinking back on the situation with Clara, it reminded me if the flooding night when we spent hours of backbreaking labor at Fife's. Most of us gay boys were raised to be polite or were born with the inherent sense of knowing the difference between right and wrong, good and evil, and even the difference between tasteful and tacky. Some smart heterosexuals recognize that and figure out how to use it, but those who abuse our good nature are as bad as those who would banish our gentle souls to the depths of hell. Both kinds of people are fools.

CHAPTER EIGHT:
From waiter to bartender

Gay men in San Francisco in the '70s and '80s lived fabulously. Rents were dirt cheap, even in the Castro, which most of the much older residents were fleeing. Young gay men were buying and fixing up property, some with money their parents had given them with the promise that they would disappear forever. Even those of us who didn't have the good sense to invest in cheap real estate had enough discretionary income to spend it on track lighting, great stereos, record collections, and recreational drugs.

The trouble with drugs and living at the river that first winter was that when the weekend ended and all my friends went back to the city, I was alone and lonesome and the knotty pine walls just laughed at me. I was ready for spring and for work to start at the fabulous Woods resort.

When spring came, I finally got to start waiting tables and earning some money. The first night I worked at The Woods was incredibly busy! I had a party of six at a round table by the fireplace in the far corner of the dining room. It seemed like every room of every building at the Russian River had its own fireplace. Three of my customers wanted soup and three of them wanted salads.

I went to the kitchen and got everything arranged onto one big round tray that I deftly carried over my head as I maneuvered my way across the busy dining room.

With my free hand I flipped open a folding stand to set the tray upon, but just as I did, one of the drunken guests at that table threw his fist into the air to express his point about something. His fist sent soup and salads and chilled forks and warmed spoons all over the place! I cleaned everything up as best I could and looked around to see all three of the owners at a table across the room, staring at me after hearing the commotion, no doubt asking each other, "Who hired *him*?"

My only waiter shifts were Friday and Saturday nights and Sunday brunch on the patio. They still used the same old kitchen that had fed the rich and famous at the Hexagon House all those years. As soon as my waiter shifts ended I usually hit the dance floor. The new sound system was amazing and the light show at night rivaled all my favorite discos in San Francisco, which in those days were Trocadero Transfer, the I-Beam, the Music Hall, and Dreamland.

As an employee, I could drink for next to nothing, so I did. I wasn't looking for a steady boyfriend, but I met dozens of sexy guys on the dance floor from all over the country and around the world. One of my favorites at the time was a guy from the city who had a VW van with a mattress in the back. At some point every Saturday night we slipped out to the parking lot for a sweaty fuck in the van. We went back in for more drinks before Last Call and rejoined all the other guys under the mirror ball on the dance floor.

California law maintained that alcohol sales had to cease at 2 a.m., but the music didn't. The bartenders always stashed a couple of bottles in the ice machine off the kitchen for after-hours, some peppermint schnapps (for fresh breath, of course) and at least one bottle of chilled Stoli vodka. The door with the sign that said STAFF ONLY never stopped me from bringing my friends and tricks back there whenever someone wanted a nip after the bar was closed.

Even when the dancing stopped, around 4 a.m., the hot tub was still bubbling away, both swimming pools were open, and lots of people had parties in their rooms or cabins. On Sunday mornings I usually crawled into work with a hangover, but I was used to doing that when I lived in the city. Brunch ended around 2 or 3 p.m. and I sometimes spread a towel beside one of the pools and dropped half a tab of acid. I knew there was nothing I had to do for the next four days until Friday night when I came back to work.

I had an old green Datsun pickup truck that was so rusted out around the floor shift you could see the road from inside the cab. Some Sundays four or five of us would pile into my truck or someone's convertible, all of us high as a kite on pot or Quaaludes or LSD or MDA or cocaine or some combination thereof. I mostly stuck with acid that first season at the River. We would tear ass down Armstrong Woods Road to Guerneville and then head out River Road to the Rusty Nail or stop in to see Sam and Jim at the Lodge, take a dip in their pool and see what was going on at their place. They threw some incredible parties at the Russian River Lodge, although I don't remember them as well as I would have, had I not been so stoned.

The General Manager who hired me at The Woods was someone named Tom, but I never saw him again after my interview. I think he'd already moved back to the city. He must have discovered how hard it was to work for three bosses who had equal shares in the business and vastly different opinions on how they wanted things done.

It seems like The Woods went through a lot of different managers during my years there. The one in charge during my first season was Chris Osborne. Chris became a very dear friend of mine in later years until he died, much too young. He was a little older than me and he came off as being pretty crazy. He had this strange, powerful energy, even without drugs. He must have been one of those children they had to keep heavily sedated while he was growing up. Now, he was full of ideas, always looking for ways to improve things that were already pretty great.

I told Chris I wanted to work as a bartender because they were the only ones making any real money on the weekends. We wouldn't be open full time—during the week—until after Memorial Day weekend. That was when the summer season unofficially started. I needed to pay the rent now.

It was on Sunday of Memorial Day weekend when I finished the brunch shift, went out to the nude pool and dropped a little acid. I crawled out onto an inflatable blue plastic air mattress and lay flat on my back in the pool. The acid was coming on gently and I was floating in a sea of blue in bliss, even though it smelled a bit like chlorine. I heard someone call my name so I looked up. It was Chris, the manager, a thousand miles away, standing at the edge of the pool. My vision was hazy, but I could see that he was beckoning me to come towards him, so I paddled across what seemed like an enormous body of water to find out what he wanted.

"Mark, we're short a bartender. Do you want to take the shift?"

"What time does it start?"

"Right now. The place is packed for tea dance and they're still pouring in. Cars must be parked halfway to Guerneville."

"Well, I wished you'd asked me before I dropped that acid when I got off work."

He laughed like he must have thought I was kidding. "Come on. I'll get you a bank and give you a crash course on how to work the register."

I pulled on my red gym shorts, a t-shirt and sneakers. Chris said, "Ditch the t-shirt. You'll make more money without it." He was right. I made nearly 200 bucks in tips that afternoon. I had never made nearly that much in a whole weekend of waiting tables. This was it!

∽

There was an old wooden shed on the patio, just off the dance floor. It had a little roof over a bar counter on the front, several shelves in the back over a refrigeration system for kegs of beer and an ancient cash register that worked without electricity. It looked like it hadn't been used in years, but Chris got it cleaned up and ready to go and he wanted me to work it, especially for Sunday T-Dance every week.

We gave it a coat of paint, stocked it with liquor, and found some extra bar stools to set around it. Chris figured out that if we sold 10 oz. paper cups of cheap domestic draft beer for 25 cents a cup, we could still make a profit. None of the indoor bars had draft beer, only bottles. We put up signs everywhere that said 25 CENT BEER on the PATIO and it was a huge hit. Guys would order one glass and leave me a dollar or order ten glasses and leave me a five or even a ten.

My bar back, Earl, was a lithe young man who was a skater and toured with ice shows during the winter months. Charles Shultz, the cartoonist who created *Peanuts*, had built an ice rink in 1969 in nearby Santa Rosa, where lots of skaters trained, and many of them found summer jobs at the gay bars, restaurants and resorts that started booming in the early '80s. I loved working with Earl because he was so flexible that he could move around me and practically under my feet without getting in my way. He was also a really sweet kid who lived with his boyfriend, a big beefy bear of a guy in a house in Rio Nido. I got into the habit of working every

Sunday T-Dance on a little bit of acid and we always had plenty of cocaine, which came in handy if either of us were lagging.

Working T-Dance was my favorite shift and I made great tips. There were a half dozen bar stools at the patio bar, but most of my drink sales were to sweat-drenched guys coming off the dance floor. I always did a little bit of LSD on Sundays, not enough to hallucinate, but just enough to make me see the humor in everything. That was the season when someone figured out how to put acid in Pez candy, so everyone carried around Pez candy dispensers which brought back fond childhood memories as well.

Laughter is infectious. I was always having fun behind the bar, so that was another reason I made great tips, besides the fact that all I ever wore was a pair of short red gym-shorts and loafers. Every now and then when it was beastly hot and I had worked up a sweat I'd tell Earl to take over for a couple of minutes, just long enough for me to run across the footbridge, pull off my shorts, kick off my shoes, and dive into the pool to cool off.

After I pulled my shorts and shoes back on and returned to work, Earl would step behind the back of the bar where the beer kegs were and chop us each a couple of lines of coke. Sundays were so much fun!

CHAPTER NINE:
Gabriel Starr and Rita Rockett

Late one afternoon Chris, the manager, and Gabriel Starr and I strung tiny white fairy lights in the trees above and around the patio bar so that when evening came on it was very festive. We were probably stoned enough to even call our work "fabulous!" We also strung lights on the footbridge over Fife Creek, so when you walked toward the dance floor from the direction of the nude pool and the cabins, it was like entering a fairyland. How gay could we get?

Gabriel was one of my fellow bartenders. He had grown up in the East Bay. I want to say Hayward, California, but I'm not sure. When Val Diamond came to perform at The Woods, it turned out that they had known each other from way back. They'd gone to high school together or maybe Gabe had a sister who was in Val's class.

Gabriel Starr was not his real name, I later discovered. He had chosen it, I never found out why. It had something to do with his father and the mob, an escape from his past. Maybe Val Diamond would know. She's retired from *Beach Blanket Babylon*, the longest running live musical revue in the world, which also closed on New Year's Eve in 2019, but Val is still around.

Gabe was one of the funniest people I knew. He loved to laugh and he loved to make me laugh and we loved working together. Before he moved to the river, he had been a bartender at the notorious Balcony on Market Street near Church Street in San Francisco. At least it was called the Balcony until the letter C fell down and nobody bothered to replace it, so everyone called it the Bal-ony from then on. They even had T-shirts made with the letter C dangling below the rest of the name. I only went there a few times but I remember the line around the block waiting to get inside when they opened at 6 a.m. on Sunday mornings. Gabe told me that each of the morning bartenders got a gram of cocaine in their opening bank so that they could relate to the customers, who were all stoned out of their minds, coming from the baths or from dancing all night at one of the many happening discos in San Francisco in the late '70s and early '80s.

We were stringing white fairy lights with a staple gun, lining the footbridge over Fife Creek and Gabriel's friend Rita Rockett was there. I was aware of the notorious Rita Rockett from a distance, but the first time we ever met was when Gabriel introduced us out on the back deck of The Woods Resort that night. I knew that Rita could usually be found dancing on the pool table at the Balcony on Market Street, yelling, "Baby, let's party!" but that night we were miles from the city, just us, Gabe and Chris and me on a warm spring evening, and then Rita too, as if Gabriel had just conjured her up out of his imagination. In later years Rita would become known as one of the angels of the AIDS ward at San Francisco General Hospital, serving Sunday brunches with great love and good cheer to all the dying patients and their visiting families for years.

Knowing Chris Osbourne, I'm sure we were passing around a joint that night, and Rita and Gabe were talking so fast and laughing so much that I couldn't get a word in, but I didn't care because it was so much fun to be with them. Rita and I discovered later that we shared a birthday. Our friendship would develop and overlap and intertwine in the following years with the porn star Al Parker, another birthday-mate, and so many wonderful characters like Rita's good friend Sylvester that it almost feels surreal now, but at the time we were just living our lives as best we could.

Sylvester performing at The Woods

CHAPTER TEN:
Sharon McNight, Sylvester, and Two Tons O' Fun

In those years before AIDS, San Francisco had dozens more gay bars than it has now. There were big discos and little piano bars and leather bars and gay restaurants and bath houses and afterhours clubs. Dozens of cabaret singers got their starts at places like Sutter's Mill, Trinity Place, the Plush Room on Nob Hill, and Fanny's on 18TH Street in the Castro. I think almost all of them did a turn at Locals' Night at The Woods. I had seen most of their acts in the city, but I got to know many of them better at the river when I became the maître'd for the Monday evening shows.

The first performer I saw at The Woods (aside from Michael Greer, back when the Hexagon House was still a restaurant, before I worked there) must have been Sharon McNight. She's got a powerful voice and great comic timing, an old-time show business pro with brass in her blood and a no-nonsense attitude about everything she does, whether material from Sophie Tucker or country/western songs or the entire encapsulated movie soundtrack of *The Wizard of Oz* in about fourteen minutes flat. Sharon and Michael Greer were friends from Provincetown where they rewrote the lyrics to the old Patti Page hit "ODD Cape Cod" with lyrics like, "If you're fond of chicken and don't mind crabs."

Unlike most of the local cabaret singers, Sharon McNight actually recorded record albums (on vinyl) and would later star on Broadway and earn a Tony Award nomination for Best Leading Actress in the musical *Starmites*. Sharon spoke of knowing Glen Milstead before most of the rest of the world knew him as Divine. She would later sing and tap dance in a gorilla costume in *Men Behind Bars* at the Victoria Theater in the Mission district and perform whenever she was asked at every street fair, Pride Parade, dog show, Christmas tree lighting and grand opening. I think it safe to say that no one has performed at more AIDS benefits than Sharon McNight.

Sharon McNight performing at The Woods

A few years later, in 1986, Sharon McNight and Rita Rockett were named Co-Grand Marshalls of the San Francisco Pride Parade because they had both worked so hard to help in the fight against AIDS. This was when the parade still had one Grand Marshall, rather than the dozens it has now. I remember some folks putting up a huge stink because these two heterosexual women were being honored when they thought it should always be someone from the LGBTQXYZ (or whatever) community. Someone always has to complain about everything!

It must have been partly through Rita that I got to know her good friend Sylvester. I got to know him better when I worked at The Woods and he performed there many times. Sylvester's birthday was September 6, but we celebrated with a birthday party for him every Labor Day weekend.

The first time we had Sylvester at The Woods was with Two Tons O' Fun, Izora Rhodes and Martha Wash. This was before they recorded "It's Raining Men" and became known as The Weathergirls. Sometimes Jeanie Tracy joined them, so Sylvester would announce his back-up singers as "Two and a half Tons O' Fun." She would also go on to provide background vocals for artists such as Aretha Franklin, Whitney Houston, and Mariah Carey. Jeanie was a total sweetheart.

Sylvester was already onstage that night and I was upstairs in the dressing room with Martha and Izora when one of them lit a joint and the three of us shared it. I could have only taken two or three good tokes when we heard Sylvester announce his two back-up singers while the disco beat kept throbbing. Martha handed me the joint and I went out to stand at the railing of the balcony, watching those two large women hustle down the spiral staircase in heels to join Sylvester on stage for "Disco Heat. They sang. They danced. They wailed with Sylvester and the crowd went wild!

I couldn't believe how stoned I was at that moment. I couldn't
have told you my name, much less spelled it, but those two women
who had smoked as much as I did were working it! I've always
been impressed with people who can hold it together better than I
can, even though I'm not sure that's supposed to be an admirable
quality, the ability to hold one's drugs. Oh, well...

I need to go back in time a little bit to explain why Sylvester
was so well loved. He had been part of the notorious Cockettes
in the early '70s, and then he cut a couple of albums with The
Hot Band including soulful renditions of "God Bless the Child,"
"Steamroller Blues," (A couple of years later I got Sylvester and Val
Diamond, when she was still the star of Beach Blanket Babylon,
to do a duet of "Steamroller Blues" one night at the SF Eagle) and
"Don't Let Me Be Lonely Tonight." He became our most beloved
hometown disco star.

Sylvester was idolized, but he always felt like one of us, too. He
was as much a part of the local gay community as Harvey Milk,
never afraid to be out and proud. Sometimes he wore enough
beads and feathers to outdo Janis Joplin in her heyday. Sometimes
he wore wigs and make-up on stage, but I didn't really think of his
as a drag queen. He was just Sylvester, one of a kind. He sang at
every disco in town and there was one summer when he performed
every Sunday afternoon at the Elephant Walk (now Harvey's) and
stopped traffic at 18TH and Castro. The windows would be wide
open and crowds spilled out into the intersection from all four
corners for the weekly free Sylvester concert.

Sylvester performed at every one of the first Castro Street
Fairs that I can remember. My first was in August of 1975, when I
had only been in San Francisco a few weeks, but Harvey Milk had
started the tradition the year before. Sylvester was always the star
of the main stage on Castro Street between the Twin Peaks bar and
the Bank of America. I think it was around five o'clock when he

came on, so my friends and I would drop a little acid around 4:15 and start to make our way toward Market Street and get as close as we could to the stage.

One year we were all really bummed out when we heard that Sylvester would *not* be at the Castro Fair. He would be in the middle of a European tour that Sunday. He was too famous for us to hold onto him anymore. He had outgrown the Elephant Walk on Castro Street and the I-Beam on Haight Street and the Trocadero Transfer and all the other clubs in San Francisco, large and small. We were happy for him, but sad for us.

We all went to the Castro Fair that day anyway, of course. We could still get together with our friends and make a day of it, drinking, eating fair food, cruising, and running into all sorts of people you didn't get to see every day. Everybody always came out for the Castro Street Fair!

By mid-afternoon I was feeling the weight of some degree of sadness that Sylvester wouldn't be there, especially in my stoned on pot state. My gang of friends and I agreed that we would follow tradition that day, regardless, so we all made our way toward the main stage to see who they got to perform in Sylvester's place. We did a little bit of acid and drank our draft beer in paper cups and waited while the DJ cranked out somebody else's disco hits. We tried to imagine who else they might have arranged to replace Sylvester and come out onto that sacred Castro Fair stage. Linda Clifford? Melba Moore? The Village People?

The announcer finally got on the microphone to end our suspense. "Ladies and gentlemen... please welcome to the stage... the one... the only... Sylvester!" He had flown back in the middle of his European tour just for us, just to do an hour (including encores) at the annual Castro Street Fair, so as not to disappoint his San Francisco family of fans and friends. We went nuts, of course, and then Sylvester got back in his limousine and went back to the airport, flew back to somewhere in Germany and went on with his tour. We all floated back to the bars or went home, if we were smart.

Martha Wash and Izora Rhodes-Armstead perform as Two Tons O' Fun at The Woods. They would later change their name to The Weathergirls with their huge disco hit "It's Raining Men."

I remember another time with Sylvester at The Woods. It had to have been New Year's Eve of either '82 or '83. We ran his sound check in the late afternoon before a group of four or five of us took Sylvester to dinner at Casa de Joanna, a wonderful Mexican restaurant on the south side of the Russian River, just a couple of blocks from where I lived. That night we were all excited because he was premiering a new song. Well, it was an old song, Freda Payne's hit "Band of Gold," but it was new to Sylvester.

After I moved back to the city, I saw Sylvester even more often, riding his little blue scooter down to Castro Street to shop at Cliff's hardware, stopping in next door to say hello when I was bartending days at the Special. It seemed like he was always on a float in the gay parade with the best sound system available at the time. And then one year, he wasn't. On Sunday, June 26, 1988, Sylvester came down Market Street in a wheelchair pushed by his manager Tim McKenna in front of a sign that read "People Living with AIDS." He wore a big black hat and white slacks, no feathers or beads. He died a few months later on December 16, but his music will live on forever. I wonder what he would have to say today about how much the spirit of the Castro has changed.

CHAPTER ELEVEN:
Food and Drink

Some summer days at the river the heat was so intense it could make you crumple. It felt even harsher than the heat on the Minnesota farm where I grew up. At least in Minnesota you might get hit with a rip-snorting thunderstorm now and then, lightning and hail, whipping winds and even a tornado. California heat is constant, especially the farther you're inland from ocean breezes.

Jonathan's house was just down the street from the second summer bridge south of Guerneville. A summer bridge is made up of large corrugated metal culverts laid down across the river with enough gravel thrown over them that a car can drive cross. They're called summer bridges because they wash out when the winter rains come. In summer, they damn the water up on one side enough that it shoots through the culverts. It felt wonderful to cool off in the waist deep water on the downstream side, letting the pressure of that powerful cascade pound down on my chest and back as I turned around in it.

Some summer days I had nothing better to do than play in the river or lie out by the pool, either the one at home on Orchard Avenue or one of the bigger pools at The Woods. Some days my friends and I would drive over to Fife's for a change of pace, lie out by their pool or sit at the bar upstairs with all the windows wide open and a blissful breeze coming through.

Gay bars had just started serving cranberry juice in the early '80s, so as bartenders we had a bunch of new drinks to make. Orange juice had been forbidden in gay bars for a while in the '70s during Anita Bryant's anti-gay crusade. Then bar owners discovered that oranges grew in California too... Orange County...hello!

The Coors Beer boycott started in the '70s too, but that one never did seem to end, maybe because most gay beer drinkers have better taste than to order that watery swill.

Vodka and cranberry juice with a squeeze of lime was called a Cape Codder, eventually shortened to Cape Cod. Vodka with orange juice had always been called a screwdriver, but when you added cranberry juice to a screwdriver you got a drink called a madras. I remember as a teenager getting plaid shirts that were made of a fabric called bleeding madras, which meant that their colors faded and Mom always had to wash them with dark clothes and keep them away from the whites.

Vodka with grapefruit juice had always been called a greyhound or when served in a salt-rimmed glass, a salty dog which makes sense because greyhound was a breed of dog even before it became the name of an economical cross-country bus line. Vodka with grapefruit and cranberry was called a sea breeze, while vodka with cranberry and pineapple juice was called a bay breeze, although pineapple juice was mostly used in piña coladas.

Some afternoons we wore bright Hawaiian shirts over to Fife's and challenged the bartender to make us drinks to match their colors using vodka and juice, during which times the bottle of blue Curacao often got involved. We would make up silly names for our new drinks, but our shirts came off soon anyway because we always ended up in the pool.

My friend and fellow-bartender Gabriel Starr was one of the most fun people I knew to hang out with. He was far more gregarious than I was. He could have a lengthy conversation with a total stranger and always leave them laughing. He also loved to go out to eat, so he knew just about every restaurant and dive in Sonoma County.

Gabriel turned me on to a place in Santa Rosa where they served great fried chicken and we always stopped for a drink at one of Santa Rosa's gay bars afterward. The Santa Rosa Inn was the larger of the two. The pale brick walls inside made me feel like I was in a Lutheran church recreation hall. All it needed was a giant cross above the pool table. I never picked up anyone there. I don't think Gabe did, either. What I remember best was that the parking lot was huge, so it must have been surrounded by a lot of other businesses that were only open during the daytime. I don't think the bar exists anymore. I guess if the best thing I can remember about a gay bar is the parking lot, it wasn't all that great.

The other bar, the smaller one, was just south of Santa Rosa at the bottom of an exit ramp going south on Highway #101. I don't remember which exit ramp or the name of the place, but it was considered a leather bar. At least the walls were covered in pictures of leather bars from various cities around the world. The building was an old Quonset hut, so it was a little claustrophobic inside with just enough room for a pool table and meat racks around the walls, a bar with a few stools and a big black iron wood-burning stove. I don't think Gabe and I ever took anyone home from there either, but we met some nice guys who lived and worked in the area and didn't care for the "Twinkie" atmosphere of the Santa Rosa Inn. We sometimes ran into friends there too, other resort staff or regular customers of ours or even people from San Francisco who wanted a taste of something different. It was different, all right. It was "cool," the way the Ambush in San Francisco's South of Market district was or the old Stud on Folsom Street or the way the Hole in the Wall Saloon has always been "cool."

Gabriel also turned me on to a great old gay restaurant on River Road east of Guerneville called Burdon's. The first time I went there I was surprised to find such a fancy white-linen place in such a country setting. It seemed to have been there forever and it felt gay, at least when we went there. I always confused the name with a place at 2223 Market Street in San Francisco called Burton's. They were similar in style, real old-fashioned dinner houses with a great bar, delicious steaks and prime rib and fresh salmon when it was in season and usually a starter course of escargot. John Preston and I used to love to go to Burton's for their Yankee Pot Roast.

Burdon's on the river was run by a couple of old queens and it was terrific. They seemed to love seeing a group of us come in. They hovered over us like proud aunties and treated us like we fit right in with their crisp linen napkins, fine china and crystal. I suppose we were special to them, so young and healthy and deeply tanned, living the time of our lives, not knowing how lucky we were not to be aware of the plague that was coming soon.

Another place we liked to eat was in Monte Rio, the next town west of Guerneville on River Road. It was called the Village Inn Resort and it wasn't necessarily a gay resort or bar or restaurant, but we could bask in Hollywood nostalgia there from a time before our own. Scenes from the 1942 film *Holiday Inn* were filmed there. That's the one in which Bing Crosby sings the Irving Berlin classic *White Christmas*. The legend goes that Bing Crosby was attending the encampment at the Bohemian Grove and didn't want to hold up filming so they trucked in a lot of snow and used the nearby Village Inn as a backdrop for the movie.

Weekdays at the Russian River could be idyllic in the ever-present fragrance of the ancient redwoods and so peaceful after most of the pretty party boys who crowded the pools and dance floors all weekend went back to the city. Some stuck around for another day or two—waiters, bartenders, and hairdressers, mostly. As the summer days grew hotter, more people rented rooms and cabins for longer stays, guys on vacation from all across the country and around the world.

It was on one of those weekdays early in the season when I joined a group of local waiters and bartenders for a day trip to a new gay resort I had never heard of before called Wildwood. We all met in front of the Rainbow that morning, a caravan of cars and pickup trucks and campers and motorcycles. I remember being impressed that some of the bartenders could afford to drive beautiful late-model convertibles and of course their tops were down on such a perfect day.

We drove west out of town on River Road for several miles until we took a right turn to the north. I was glad that someone in the lead knew where we were going. The road wound through dark canyons of redwoods, steeper and narrower as we climbed. It was only one lane wide in some places and deeply rutted at times. It would be barely navigable during the heavy winter rains, but we finally reached the top and the views were gorgeous!

This mountaintop place had over 200 acres of footpaths for hiking or horseback riding. I think I remember a rubber tire tree swing at Julie Andrews Point, so named because the view from there was as vast as those opening scenes from the 1965 movie *The Sound of Music* when she spins round and round and sings the title song. A few of those butch River bartenders turned into silly queens that day, at least long enough to spread their arms and take a few spins themselves.

There was a big house with an enormous kitchen and nearby was a beautiful swimming pool. We spent most of my day there, drinking beer and passing joints around, going in for an occasional dip in the most crystal clear blue water I had ever seen, but that might have been the result of the marijuana. It was a wonderful place to make some new friends at the start of my first season on the River.

They fed us very well, too. In hindsight, I realize that they hoped we would tell others about this place, so far removed from the bustle of the little town of blossoming gayness far below. What a sensible way to advertise. I never did make it back up there, but I told my customers about it again and again.

Mark at the front door of the blue house on Orchard Avenue

CHAPTER TWELVE:
The sex life of bartenders

I was only 28 years old when I moved up north to the Russian River and still just as horny as the teenaged farm boy I once was. During five years of living in the San Francisco of the wild and carefree gay '70s, I was accustomed to having sex whenever I wanted it. Now I found myself in a whole new environment and realized that things were going to be different. I never even considered going without sex. I just knew I was going to have to work a little harder to find it. There were no bathhouses in Guerneville! The nearest adult book store with a video arcade was twenty miles away in Santa Rosa. That sort of thing was always rather hit and miss anyway and never really my scene.

When I started working at The Woods, just waiting tables on the weekends, I was able to pick up guys after my shift ended. The kitchen closed on Friday and Saturday nights long before the dance floor and the bars did. On Sundays, my brunch shift always ended in plenty of time for me to play around all afternoon.

Once I started bartending, I was stuck behind the bar until 2 a.m. and then I had closing duties, stocking and balancing my bank and counting my tips, so I might not be free until 2:30 or later.

Gabriel offered me his advice. He told me that whenever he met a potential date across the bar, in order to see whether or not the guy was serious about hooking up, Gabe would tell him, "Fine, but from now until closing time, you're drinking coffee!" That usually thinned out any potential partners pretty quickly. I never even considered trying his method. I figured most of us used drugs to stay up late at that age and I never even needed boner pills to get it up, no matter how many recreational drugs I had imbibed. Ah, youth!

One night I met a guy across the bar who wanted to come over after I got off work. I had seen him earlier that afternoon right after he drove up from the city. He parked in the lot out by the nude pool, a baby blue Mustang convertible with the top down. I was standing inside the wooden fence that surrounded the pool, smoking a cigarette, watching what was going on, the weekly influx of Friday flight from the cares of city life, men arriving for the weekend, pouring into Guerneville with their cars and campers and pickup trucks and motorcycles.

This guy was hot! Hairy-chested and shirtless, solidly built and handsome, he had pale blue eyes almost the color of his car. I lost track of him for a few hours, but that night he showed up at my bar several times and was obviously flirting with me. At one point both of us leaned across the bar, fingered each other's nipples and finally kissed.

It is indeed possible to communicate so very much in a short time, with smiles and eye contact and four hands reaching across a bar made of redwood like the trees outside, tugging gently at four nipples and a kiss, just long enough to want more… to need more.

And if nothing more came of it than sex, if he turned out to be a closeted Catholic priest with a pencil dick and stinky feet or worse, one of those hideous self-loathing gay Republicans, at least I was going to have sex and that would have to be enough. Then on with the show...*next*! I saw a sign outside a pizzeria on Castro Street that said, "Sex is like pizza. When it's good it's really good. When it's not, it's still pretty good."

It was all very quick, sweet, and friendly with this guy whose name I don't remember. I didn't have time to stop pouring drinks and opening beers. I had to make my weekend tips. I took just enough time to write down my address and draw a little map on a trick pad with instructions on how to get to my house on Orchard Avenue, plus my phone number, just in case he got lost. He left before I did, at last call, said something about wanting to stop back at Fife's, where he'd rented a cabin for the weekend, needed to pick up some poppers or lube or something.

When I got off work I hurried to get out of there. The dance floor would still be jumping for hours. The parking lots were jam packed and there were vehicles lined up on both sides of Armstrong Woods Road halfway to town. I was headed south toward home when I noticed the flashing red lights of two police cars just before I got to Guerneville. Then I saw the blue convertible and my potential playmate, still shirtless on this hot summer night, the red lights splashing across the sweat on his hairy chest, his arms in the air, fingertip to nose, walking a straight line. I'd seen enough cop shows to know that I'd better keep right on driving.

What else could I do? Get arrested with him? People had warned me that the cops in Sonoma County were fierce on nailing drunk drivers all along River Road and my trick hadn't even gotten that far yet. Next he would have to ride to Santa Rosa in the back of a police car while his convertible was towed into storage somewhere. He would be booked into jail and have to spend at least that night behind bars. He might be stuck there until Monday when there was a judge in the courtroom. Then he would have to spend thousands of dollars before he could get his life back to normal.

I had been so ready to get naked with that guy! Now I was frustrated as all hell, but the sight of those flashing red lights had scared me enough to go straight home. I could feel sorry for myself from the comfort of my own sweet bed instead of a jail cell. I never saw that guy or his pretty blue convertible again.

I used to tell my friends who were not in the bar/restaurant business: "Never date a bartender!" because of their strange hours. It almost felt like we were living an opposite life from the rest of the working world. When our friends were playing, we were working. When they were toiling at their dull 9-5 jobs, we had long luxurious days to soak up the sun and swim and drink frozen daiquiris beside the pool.

Most of the guests who checked into the rooms and cabins at The Woods during the week were guys on vacation. They came from all over the world to check in for a week or two and explore the Russian River area, the nearby wine country, and the Sonoma coast. Couples usually preferred a cabin to a hotel room. The cabins were out back near the nude pool, hot tub, and parking lot. There was also an odd little greenhouse out there. It had been abandoned for years with nothing but weeds growing up from the dirt floor and a few broken clay pots. The windows were filthy and green with moss.

One time we put an old bathtub in the greenhouse for a "leather weekend" party for guys into water sports. Ken, the partner of Gene, who was one of the three owners of The Woods, cleaned up the old greenhouse and started raising chickens in there, fancy ones, "show hens," I guess he called them. Ken was quite a character, lanky and blond and very sexy, I thought, with a shy "aw-shucks" demeanor that reminded me of John Boy from *The Waltons* TV series.

I decided that I should amend my own advice to my friends to say, "Never date a bartender…unless you are one." I never dated a co-worker at The Woods, not a bartender, anyway. There was one guy they hired to do some kind of construction, expanding one of the decks, maybe. He was fun! I dated a bartender from the Rainbow Cattle Company a few times. Midweek, on one of our days off, we drove out to Jenner at the mouth of the Russian River for lunch overlooking the ocean. Jenner-by-the-Sea always sounded to me like the most romantic name for a coastal village that exists anywhere on earth.

Sometimes I took dates to Goat Rock Beach just south of Jenner and other times we headed north to the Timber Cove Inn. Beside it stands an enormous sculpture, the "Peace Obelisk" by Benjamino Bufano. Inside, we would drink Irish Coffees beside a fireplace so huge you could stand up inside it, especially in the winter when we could watch storm clouds roll across the Pacific and angry waves crashing beneath us. I went there with lots of different boyfriends. I'm not sure what happened with that bartender from the RBCC. He was fun and very sexy. Maybe he moved back to the city. Not everyone can take the country life after a while.

I dated a bartender from Fife's Resort for a season. His name was Michael and we had almost the exact same schedule, so he was always available to do things together. He drove a motorcycle, but we usually took my pickup truck when we wanted to go someplace together. One day we drove to the coast and north beyond Timber Cove. We got totally lost on gravel back roads above Highway 1. It didn't matter. We had all the time in the world.

I remember coming upon a riot of bright colors through the trees in the distance up ahead. When we got closer a building took shape, some kind of temple, surrounded by tall fences so we couldn't get too close. Michael said he thought it was the Buddhist monastery where (then and future) Governor Jerry Brown sometimes visited. He was nicknamed "Governor Moonbeam" because of his interest in both the Jesuits and Zen.

It was a steamy hot summer day, especially as we drove further away from the ocean. I pulled over in the truck and stopped beside a little bridge where we both got out to stretch a little. We looked down, saw a stream far below us, and decided to climb down there to cool off. We left our clothes on some rocks and went skinny dipping in the beautiful clear cool water.

It was bliss! Michael and I wandered downstream a ways to a spot out of view of the bridge, even though we never heard another vehicle the whole time we were down there. The stream widened out into a perfect blue pool surrounded by sun-bleached white boulders.

Michael might have been a couple of years older than me, maybe in his early thirties. I remember him as hairy and handsome with a dark complexion and a deep voice. The water felt magical and I'm sure we were high on grass, at least, and it felt like we were in a scene from a porn film. Two horny naked guys, lost in the country, coming across a sunlit pond on a hot day…what better idea could we have come up with than to get naked and fuck?

CHAPTER THIRTEEN:
Locals' Night

Monday nights at The Woods remained Locals' Night, but the entertainment moved from the side dining room where my friend Bill and I had seen Michael Greer a few years earlier, into the hexagon-shaped room which was now a dance floor. We hauled in cocktail tables and chairs for the front rows, larger tables in the mid-range and picnic tables for large parties in the back. There really weren't any bad seats.

One Monday afternoon I was hanging out at The Woods when I noticed a very large man of 6′ 6″ checking in with a lot of luggage. Most guests might have a few pairs of pants or shorts and summer shirts, maybe a different swimsuit for each day of their stay, but I couldn't imagine this big guy in a Speedo. I heard him say that his name was Don McLean and that he was expected. I didn't figure out until that evening that Don McLean was also known as Lori Shannon, a headliner at the world famous Finocchio's nightclub on Broadway in San Francisco.

I must confess that my knowledge of gay history when I was in my twenties was not what it is now. Lori Shannon was the drag queen who played Edith Bunker's good friend Beverly LaSalle on three episodes of Norman Lear's groundbreaking 1970s sitcom *All in the Family* who was eventually killed in a gay-bashing, leading to "Edith's Crisis of Faith," which was the title of that episode. On stage at The Woods, Lori Shannon came off as warm and loving, much like the character of Beverly LaSalle, and a very funny comedienne. I also realized all that luggage had been full of gowns and shoes and wigs and make-up and feather boas. Don McLean died in 1984 at the age of 45 and I was very glad that I once got to meet him and see his act.

Advertisement in the *Bay Area Reporter* (early '70s)

Somehow, I soon ended up in charge of assigning the cocktail waiters to their sections for Locals' Night, being the liaison between the performers and the sound and light guys, and acting as maître d' on those Monday nights, marking the tables where people had made reservations and seating everyone as the audience arrived. We moved a large portable stage into place in front of the huge stone fireplace with a spinet piano beside it.

No matter how debauched my weekends were, I always looked forward to Monday nights—"Locals' Nights"—which drew far more people than just those who lived on the river, especially during the height of the tourist season.

San Francisco had many clubs with live entertainment in those days and plenty of great cabaret performers. I had seen nearly all of them at some point at Trinity Place or Sutter's Mill in the financial district or at Fanny's in the Castro. The city was filled with talents like Sharon McNight, Gail Wilson, Ruth Hastings, Meg Mackay and dozens of others. Most of them made at least one trip up north to perform at The Woods, if not an annual appearance.

Samantha Samuels was one of the owners' favorites, a tiny woman who sounded like Edith Piaf and tried to channel the "Little Sparrow" on stage. I guess she was pretty good at it, but Piaf was never my cup of tea. I preferred the brassy, ballsy singers. If Edith Piaf had still been alive and made a trip in person to perform at the Russian River, I suspect that I wouldn't have been much more enthused about her than I was about her impersonator.

Samantha Samuels had a gay manager who was also her brother-in-law, I think. I remember one time she couldn't make it to the afternoon sound check before her show—stuck in traffic, or something—and this manager said, "No problem. I can do it for her." He stood on the stage where she would be that night and he sang one of her Piaf numbers and sounded almost like her. The creepy part was that he also made every gesture that Samantha would use that night, every tip of the head, every hand movement; he had every bit of her act down pat. When I realized how meticulously choreographed her entire shtick was, I was amazed that she left not an inch of room for any spontaneity.

I liked Nicholas, Glover, and Wray a lot! They were a female singing trio with tight harmonies, great energy and humor. They once toured with Barbara Cook and won four Cabaret Gold Awards and two Cable Car Awards. My favorite bit of trivia about them was that Willow Wray's great aunt was Fay Wray, the actress who starred opposite the ape in the original 1933 movie version of *King Kong*.

Pam Brooks was a lovely blonde soprano with perfect lip-liner. I must not have seen women wearing lip-liner before because hers really intrigued me. There's a mention of her in the book called *They Left Their Hearts in San Francisco* descending the grand staircase of San Francisco's City Hall singing the old Tony Bennett chestnut.

David Kelsey performed one Monday night at The Woods. I had first seen him on Polk Street when I was 23 years old and new in town. My old college friend Mia was visiting me from Minneapolis and we stopped in at the New Bell Saloon on a Sunday afternoon. We got our drinks from the bartender, Wayne Friday, whom I would get to know well in later years, and worked our way through the crowd toward the stage where David Kelsey was playing both a piano and an organ. He thought we were a young straight couple who had wandered into a gay bar by mistake. Mia and I played along as David got raunchier, pulling out dildos and crazy hats. We pretended to be shocked and the crowd ate it up. We were probably a little drunk, too, having just come from bar-hopping at Buzzby's or the N'Touch up the street

I did a little research on David Kelsey and discovered that after getting out of the service in 1965, he returned to San Francisco and played at several gay dinner clubs including On The Levee (987 Embarcadero) with the great Michelle (Michael Geary,) The Big Basket (238 Columbus), and Page One (431 Natoma). He did benefits for the S.I.R. Center and accompanied Empress I, Jose Sarria, the Widow Norton, for a time when Jose did his opera take-offs at the Black Cat in North Beach and Charles Pierce at Bimbo's (365 Columbus) in 1971.

According to *Vector*, the local gay rag at the time, Kelsey counted Eartha Kitt, Barbara Cook, Johnny Ray and Lauren Bacall as fans, and they often made a special effort to see him when they were in town.

In the early '80s, David Kelsey put together a small group of musicians he recruited from the Gay Freedom Day marching band to play Dixieland jazz. They performed under the name David Kelsey and Pure Trash.

About half of our Monday night cabaret performers came from San Francisco. Others were touring the country at the time or we flew them up from Los Angeles. For every local Ruth Hastings or Val Diamond (one of my favorites, even before she was the star of *Beach Blanket Babylon* for so many years,) we imported an Edith Massey or a Morgana King or a Carmen McRae.

A singer named Amanda McBroom did her cabaret act at The Woods one summer. She was best known as the songwriter who wrote "The Rose," the theme song from Bette Midler's first Oscar-nominated role in the 1979 movie of the same name. McBroom drew a big crowd, no doubt in part because of everyone's love for that song and that film, but she was no Bette Midler. McBroom had a beautiful, delicate voice, but her stage presence was so joyless that I don't remember anything else she sang that night. She was a one-time-only act at The Woods.

Long before *American Idol* or *the* Voice or *America's Got Talent*, there was a television program on Saturday nights called *Star Search*. It was where Rosie O'Donnell got her big break. The host of the show was Ed McMahon, best known as the announcer on *The Tonight Show* for decades, the one who yelled "Here's Johnny!" every weeknight to introduce Johnny Carson. *Star Search* launched the careers of many of today's household names and also showcased then unknown performers who didn't win, such as Justin Timberlake, Britney Spears and Beyoncé.

The first big *Star Search* winner for male vocalist was Sam Harris, who came to perform at The Woods, fresh off winning the $100,000 prize, landing a record deal, and appearing on *The Oprah Winfrey Show* to sing a duet with Oprah. The Monday night of

Sam's appearance, there were about twelve people in the audience, counting the owners and me. He sang his heart out, anyway. The candles were lit. The piano player was there to back him up. The show went on!

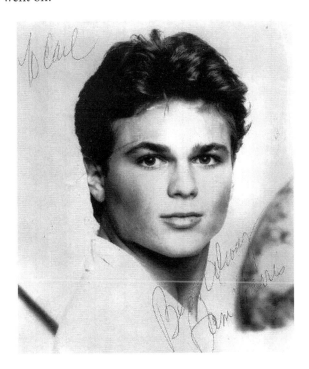

Sam Harris from *Star Search*

He was so cute, I thought, and so very gay! I'm usually attracted to bigger guys, like myself, but there was just something so endearing about him in his little shoes and his little pants and his little shirt. I felt like a pederast. He was barely old enough to buy a drink at a bar, but what a voice! He's the only singer I've heard besides Patti LaBelle to do "Over the Rainbow" with what seems like a three-octave slide on one syllable at the climax. Some would call their versions histrionic and overdone, but I loved it at the time.

I would love to have had a climax with Sam Harris that night after the show, but he was terribly closeted in those days, at least professionally. I waited for him out in the hot-tub, but someone else came along first. Sam Harris is still going strong, married to a man named Danny with whom he adopted a son named Cooper in 2008. He is now proudly, openly gay, so gay he's best friends with Liza Minnelli, for crying out loud!

CHAPTER FOURTEEN:
The Stud and
Hamburger Mary's Russian River Retreat

Some of the biggest and most profitable gay bars in San Francisco had a tradition of giving their employees the extra bonus of an annual overnight—or longer—trip to somewhere like Palm Springs or the Russian River. One time Gabriel and I got the chance to work at an unforgettable one together. It was a Monday night just before the official season started, so we were both happy to earn some extra money.

This particular retreat involved two major gay establishments footing the bill for all their employees to stay at The Woods. Gabe and I were thrilled to hear that they were coming from Hamburger Mary's and The Stud. Gabriel knew several of them already, but then, he knew everybody from having worked at The Balcony.

There was only one Hamburger Mary's in those days, the original one on Folsom Street since 1972. It had its own bar inside called Cissy's Goodtime Saloon with its own entrance next door, which was later moved around the corner onto 12TH Street. The original Stud was just across Folsom Street from Hamburger Mary's and a few doors down. These were a couple of the most fun places in the city, hippie funky dives in the midst of heavy leather bars.

Hamburger Mary's became even more popular due to frequent mentions in Herb Caen's column in the *San Francisco Chronicle* newspaper. Society ladies started coming for lunch in their furs and jewels and you might find a table of four of them seated next to a table of hungover leather queens. Caen announced in his column that Thursdays at Hamburger Mary's were "High Heels Day" and that anyone who came in high heels—"men included"—got their first drink on the house. Divine once ate there with a group of friends, got up in the middle of the meal and went outside to throw up at the curb. The staff of Hamburger Mary's treated that occasion as a christening.

I almost always saw a character at the front of the corner, just inside the door of Hamburger Mary's, who went by the name Artista. He was a chubby boy in a simple dress like my mother would have worn when she was doing housework and didn't care how she looked.

The Stud across the street was equally relaxed in terms of dress code or lack thereof. The crowd there was androgynous and sexy at the same time. Drugs were plentiful, the air was filled with tobacco and pot smoke, but it still felt like the sort of place where you could bring your visiting cousin from back home if she was cool, or better yet, if she was a conservative and you wanted to shock her.

I was asking someone just the other day what he remembered about those places. He told me he always went to Hamburger Mary's when he was coming down off an acid trip because they served such huge portions of wonderful, heavy, "hippie-fried" food. Those were the days where everywhere you went to eat in San Francisco they put alfalfa sprouts on your sandwich, even on a hamburger, and I always had to pick them off.

Eggs Benedict was three slices of whole wheat toast topped with three poached eggs drowning in plentiful perfect hollandaise sauce. I hate it when places don't give you enough hollandaise and you have to ask for more and they treat you like you're asking for the blood of their firstborn or something.

I had a favorite waiter at Hamburger Mary's for years. I don't remember his name, but he was very handsome with beautiful long straight brown hair like James Taylor or Jackson Browne, two of my favorite male singers and sex-symbols of that era. This gorgeous waiter always wore baggy tank tops that showed off his amazing body, but also showed off a scar that went in sort of a spiral around most of his torso. No one I knew ever dared to ask him about it, but the way he owned it and showed it off made him all the more sexy.

I don't remember whether that waiter was at the retreat at The Woods, but there were dozens of sexy long-haired guys there that Monday night. Gabriel and I worked the main bar. He was on the side that faced the dance floor and I was at a right angle from him on the side that faced the pool tables, coat check, and big screen TV.

All their drinks were free. We just had to ring them up on our cash registers, but not take any money. At the end of the night we turned in our tapes to one of our bosses and they would settle up later. The hosts tipped us generously too, plus paid our hourly wages and hired the DJ and light man. Gabe and I even told the partiers, our "customers," that everything was on the house and even the tip was covered. They tipped us anyway, not just with cash, but all night long they gave us joints and little white paper packets of cocaine. It's been years since I've had coke, but just writing about that night I can almost taste it on my tongue and remember how the back of my throat would go numb for a while.

Gabriel and I found a square mirror tile like the ones some people put on their walls. We set it right between our two registers and chopped and snorted lines whenever we felt like it. I don't know who had the straight-edge razor blade with them, but we had plenty of straws right in front of us. The short red ones worked the best.

12TH and Folsom Streets—San Francisco

Gabriel always cracked me up, especially when we got to work together. We would pick out someone in the crowd and do a running commentary on them, concoct an imaginary story about who they were, where they came from, how they did their job, and what they liked to do in bed.

Gabe and I both knew that if we, the bartenders, were having fun, the crowd would have even more fun. It was contagious, especially the more they drank. A good bartender never looks like he doesn't want to be there, even if he doesn't. That night was one of the best times I ever had bartending. I don't remember how it ended, whether we had to stop serving alcohol at 2 a.m. The party probably went on until 4. They didn't need much more alcohol at that point. We had probably served more bottles of water than beer and more glasses of sodas or juices than mixed drinks, especially toward the end of the night.

I wish I could tell a good story about bringing someone home to Orchard Avenue afterward for fantastic sex, but if I did I don't remember it. It's more likely that I went out and sat in the hot tub for a while, let the jets of water pound on the tight muscles of my back and shoulders while I kept one eye on my pants on the shelf, knowing there was a lot of cash and cocaine in the pockets.

NIGHT LIFE

Sarah DASH

SARAH DASH, OF LABELLE FAME, WILL BE
AT THE TROCADERO TRANSFER ON SATURDAY
MAY 28th AND THEN WILL HEAD TO THE
RIVER WHERE JUST ABOUT EVERYONE ELSE
WILL BE FOR HER SHOW AT THE WOODS ON

CHAPTER FIFTEEN:
Saturday Night Divas

There is no way that I could remember all of the performers who came to The Woods, but it seemed like every Saturday night of the summer season, every one-hit wonder appeared on the stage above the dance floor and did both the "A" and "B" sides of their disco records. Their average fee was usually around $500, if I remember correctly.

Vicki Sue Robinson came to sing "Turn the Beat Around," arriving in the afternoon for sound check with her mother in tow, a total yenta, such a caricature of a native New Yorker and stage mother combined, it was funny to listen to her talk. Vicki Sue had also sung background on Irene Cara's hit *Fame*, but I was most impressed by the fact that I had once seen her live in the cast of the Broadway musical *Hair*.

Cynthia Manley came to The Woods to perform her hit "Can't Take My Eyes Off Of You" with her backup singers, the Boystown Gang. It turned out I already knew one of them back in San Francisco in the late '70s. I met Bruce in mid-November one year, both of us in our 20s and single, and we decided to date just through the holidays. That way whenever either of us got invited to a party we would have someone to go with. We ended it amicably on New Year's Day. I'm sure he would agree that the sex wasn't that great anyway. He's the one on the right in their YouTube video, which looks ridiculously dated today. The choreography is as wooden as it gets, but the two shirtless boys in tight Levis and black leather vests still look cute.

Debbie Jacobs came to The Woods to perform her hits "High on Your Love," "Undercover Lover," and "Hot Hot."

Claudja Barry did "Down And Counting" and one of my favorite hits of the disco era "Boogie Woogie Dancin' Shoes." That was one of those songs that had made me hit the dance floor every time the DJs played it at Alfie's, the I Beam, Trocadero, The Music Hall, Bones, or Oil Can Harry's, throughout my 20s in San Francisco, so I was thrilled to hear it live. The funny thing is, some of those old disco hits were created in studios with synthesizers and so many over-dubs that when a performer sang her hits "live" we were really listening to a tape recording of a lot of background beats. In those cases, the performer had to do little more than dance around and mouth the words into a live mike. Still, it was nice to meet Claudja Barry in person.

Linda Clifford was also an actress who appeared in *Rosemary's Baby* and *Sweet Charity*, but was best known for her disco hits "Runaway Love" and "Red Light."

When Mary Wells came to The Woods, we made a party out of it and had T-shirts made that said "My Guy" across the front. I thought it seemed a little odd to call yourself your own "guy" on a shirt, but no one had asked me what I thought. It must have been Steve Mart's idea. He was the lighting designer for the disco and he planned a lot of the parties, at least the ones I didn't, but I'll get to that later.

I felt kind of sorry for Mary Wells. She came to sound check with a big black man who seemed really abusive toward her. I didn't know whether he was her husband or her "manager/pimp" or her bodyguard, but he treated her with no respect, just as he treated the rest of us. He was clearly not happy to be in a gay club.

Mary Wells, with several million-selling singles, had once been hailed as "the first lady of Motown," but she looked pathetic at my first sight of her. She had on an ill-fitting house dress and a worse-fitting wig. It was pulled back so far that it revealed a line of gray hair across her forehead. That night when she came back out to perform, she changed into something sparkly, but the wig was still the same. I couldn't understand why she hadn't looked at herself in a mirror when she changed. Besides "My Guy," she sang her most recognizable hits, "You Beat Me to the Punch," "Two Lovers," and "The One Who Really Loves You."

A few years later, in 1991, Mary Wells sued Motown Records for royalties she felt she had not received upon leaving them in 1964. Motown eventually settled giving her a six-figure sum. That same year, she testified before Congress to encourage government funding for cancer research. She died of cancer in 1992.

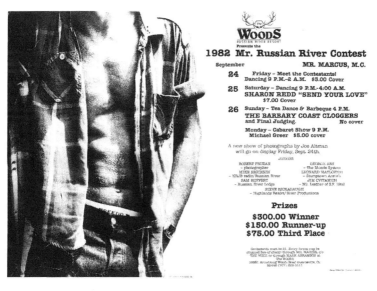

WOODS
RUSSIAN RIVER RESORT
Presents the

1982 Mr. Russian River Contest

September   MR. MARCUS, M.C.

24 Friday – Meet the Contestants!
        Dancing 9 P.M.–2 A.M. $3.00 Cover

25 Saturday – Dancing 9 P.M.–4:00 A.M.
        SHARON REDD "SEND YOUR LOVE"
        $7.00 Cover

26 Sunday – Tea Dance & Barbeque 4 P.M.
        THE BARBARY COAST CLOGGERS
        and Final Judging.   No cover

        Monday – Cabaret Show 9 P.M.
        Michael Greer $5.00 cover

A new show of photographs by Joe Altman
will go on display Friday, Sept. 24th.

JUDGES

ROBERT FRIZAN   GEORGE ASH
 – photographer   – The Muscle System
MIKE ERICKSON   LEONARD MATLOVICH
 – KRoB radio/Russian River – Stamptown Annie's
SAM HOFFERT   JIM CVITANICH
 – Russian River Lodge   – Mr. Leather of S.F. 1982
        STEVE RICKABAUGH
 – Highlands Resort/River Productions

Prizes

$300.00 Winner
$150.00 Runner-up
$75.00 Third Place

Contestants must be 21. Entry forms may be
obtained free of charge through MR. MARCUS, c/o
THE WOODS or through MARK ABRAMSON at
The WOODS
16881 Armstrong Woods Road, Guerneville, Ca.
95446 (707) 869-0111

CHAPTER SIXTEEN:
The Mister Russian River Contest

B.A.R. clipping of the winner and runners up

H aving lived in San Francisco for a few years before I moved north to the river, I knew that the gay community was big on contests, titles, and pageantry. Jose Sarria had named himself the first Empress of San Francisco in the 1960s and Marcus Hernandez, who wrote a weekly column for the *Bay Area Reporter* under the name "Mister Marcus," became the first Emperor a few years later. Those titles eventually spread to dozens of cities or "Empires" all over the United States, Canada, and Mexico.

Then came the Grand Dukes and Duchesses, Miss Gay and Mister Gay, Imperial Princes and Princesses, Czarinas, Knights, Viscounts, and Ladies-in-Waiting. Some of those were honorary titles bestowed upon the chosen few, but the big ones all involved elaborate campaigns, public voting, grand coronations, and investitures. There was even a local brewery that tried to capitalize on the gay beer-drinking market with a Mister Acme Beer contest that drew more than thirty contestants!

Toward the end of the 1982 season at The Woods, I came up with the idea of starting the Mister Russian River Contest. It was not in any way endorsed by or affiliated with the Imperial Council, but I got Mister Marcus to come up from the city and emcee the weekend of events, which ensured lots of free advertising in his column. I had a lot of fun with that project, lining up judges and contestants and entertainment for that weekend, including the Barbary Coast Cloggers, Michael Greer, and Sharon Redd.

Sharon Redd never publicly came out, but seemed comfortable in a gay environment, having performed with Bette Midler. I had seen her before we met at The Woods when she performed at Bimbo's 365 Club in San Francisco, along with Charlotte Crossley, & Ula Hedwig in *An Intimate Evening With Bette*. This iteration of Bette Midler's three backup "girls" had also released an album called *Formerly of the Harlettes*, in late 1977. Sharon was a tiny woman with a searing soprano voice who had disco hits with "Can You Handle It?" "Beat the Street" and my favorite "In the Name of Love." Sharon Redd was the Saturday night disco act on the same weekend when Michael Greer was the "Locals' Night" cabaret performer.

I remember that Michael and Sharon and I ended up in her hotel room with my good friend Bob after Michael Greer's show

Monday night. Sharon was lying in bed under a dark blue summer blanket. I was sitting on the side of the bed and Bob and Michael were in upholstered chairs. Sharon had a pile of little white envelopes on the bedside table. She would open one at a time, take a snort through a straw, and pass it on. We didn't even bother pouring the cocaine out onto a mirror and cutting it into lines with a razor blade or a credit card, the customary method. We each just stuck the straw in the envelope, snorted, and passed it along. I don't know where she had gotten all these drugs, but for whatever reason, they weren't all the same. I remember at least a couple of times when the envelope got back to her, she did another snort, said, "I don't know about you guys, but I think this one is *shit!*" and tossed the envelope across the bed to let it land on the floor.

Michael Greer had an early flight back to LAX that morning and Bob had offered to drive him down to SFO, so they decided that they might as well stay up all night. After a few snorts of coke, I decided that I might as well stay up with them and go along for the ride. By the time we left for the airport, the sun was coming up and the blue blanket on Sharon's bed was as white as a powdered sugar donut. I barely remember that early morning drive down highway 101 in the back of Bob's Jeep with the top down. Bob drove and Michael sat in the passenger seat and the three of us chain-smoked cigarettes all the way down through the city and out to the airport. Cocaine always made me crave nicotine too.

How do I even know that Sharon Redd was a lesbian? Could I have dreamt it? No, I remember knowing her wife/lover/manager, another small black woman whose name was Ruth. I'm sure I booked Sharon to perform somewhere again after I moved back to the city. Maybe at Chaps on 11TH and Harrison? I can still hear her sweet voice soaring over the instrumental track in a crowded leather bar. "Love Insurance… you're not alone… pick up the phone…" And we sent Christmas cards back and forth every year:

"To Mark with love, Sharon and Ruth"

"To Sharon and Ruth, Happy Holidays! Hugs and kisses... Mark"

Maybe we did so many drugs in those days that we all just imagined that we were friends. Sharon Redd died on May 1, 1992 of pneumonia at age 46. *Dance Music Report* magazine said that her death was AIDS-related.

Speaking of cocaine... I remember another time when Al, one of the owners, threw a dinner party at his cabin for Michael Greer when he was performing at The Woods. Michael used to come and stay for a few days before and after his shows, so we all got to be friends with him. He and Al would have been the only guys over thirty at this dinner party.

Al had been in the kitchen all day preparing several courses of his favorite Italian specialties. There were six or eight of us at the dinner table, candles lit, the first wine course poured, ashtrays cleared, ready for the soup course, when one of Al's guests, the youngest of all of us, piped up with, "Before we start, I have a little contribution to make to our dinner party. I just bought us a whole gram of coke!"

If I'd had any sense, I would have said, "Thank you, that's very generous, but why don't we put that away until after dinner, shall we? I'm sure we would all enjoy it more with our brandies and coffee."

But *no*. Nobody said anything of the kind. All any of us could hear was: "Free cocaine!" A mirror suddenly appeared and the kid dumped out the whole gram, chopped it all into nice even lines and the mirror was passed around the table until we'd snorted all of it up our noses. Ashtrays reappeared and cigarettes were lit, glasses lifted.

Needless to say, Al's day of cooking was wasted on all of us. We barely picked at our food, trying to make compliments to the chef, but not really tasting anything. I'm sure we all woke up hungry the next morning, if we were even able to get to sleep that night. Nobody likes to eat on cocaine! That's the last thing they want to do.

Someone asked me once what was my favorite thing to do on cocaine and I had the perfect answer: "More cocaine!" I guess I could have said sex… or cigarettes, which ran a close second and third, but not Italian food, even with crusty garlic bread and home made minestrone.

Michael Greer died of lung cancer on December 14, 2002 at age 63.

CHAPTER SEVENTEEN:
Guerneville

I loved to go exploring on my days off from The Woods. The country roads were lined with signs advertising ashtrays and other souvenirs made of redwood burl and later in the season there were fruit stands with a bounty of cherries and apples and melons. I became interested in the history of that part of the country where I now lived. I learned about how Northern California once had a complex network of train lines carrying passengers and cargo across the state. The North Pacific Coast narrow gauge railway line took wealthy San Franciscans from the ferry landing in Sausalito—even before the Golden Gate Bridge was built—to their summer homes along the Russian River.

During the years of the Big Band Era, all the greats came to perform for the guests on the dance floors of the big hotels and nightclubs that popped up in the River towns from Rio Nido to Jenner and as far north as Cazadero, too. They hosted such notables as Frank Sinatra, Dean Martin, Count Basie, Glen Miller, Woody Herman, and many more.

In the 1950s, Guerneville was inundated with biker gangs and by the '60s the hippies took over. When I moved there in 1981 it was turning into the Fire Island of the west coast with so many gays

opening resorts and bars and restaurants and stores to cater to the
new clientele. I learned that the Russian River Resort area swelled
every time the general U.S. economy was weaker and ebbed when
Bay Area people were able to afford travel to Hawaii, Europe, and
other more expensive vacation destinations.

In 1981, Leonard Matlovich opened a pizza parlor on Main
Street called Stumptown Annie's. The pizza was pretty good and
he was always friendly and rather shy, I thought, as he made his
way around the room to visit with the customers and make sure
that they were enjoying themselves. I had first heard of him when
he was on the cover of *Time* in 1975, the same year I moved from
Minneapolis to San Francisco. He was pictured in military gear
with the caption "I Am a Homosexual."

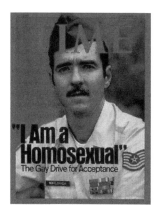

Leonard Matlovich on the cover of *Time*

He had enlisted in the Air Force when he was 19 and served
three tours of duty in Vietnam, receiving both a Bronze Star and
Purple Heart. Leonard Matlovich was among the first to volunteer
to fight the ban on gays in the military and would soon fight against
AIDS and for LGBT equality. Before he later died of AIDS a few

years later on June 22, 1988, he designed his own tombstone for the Congressional Cemetery in Washington, D.C., which doesn't bear his name because he wanted it to be a memorial to all gay veterans. It reads: "When I was in the military they gave me a medal for killing two men and a discharge for loving one."

A few doors down the street from Stumptown Annie's, Christian Haren opened a candy store. He had been a successful Broadway actor, appeared in several films for MGM, and was one of several models who portrayed "The Marlboro Man" on cigarette ads in magazines. Christian had been the manager of the Palm Springs area's popular gay club CC Construction Co and was later recognized by *Newsweek* as a leader in AIDS prevention efforts among high school and college students. I think he was the only Marlboro Man to die of AIDS instead of lung cancer.

Other shops opened in Guerneville to provide the latest in swimwear and sunglasses, along with T-shirts, suntan lotions, rolling papers, lighters and lube. The local gays, who had moved to the river first, no longer had to drive all the way down to Castro, Polk Street or SOMA to buy their cock rings and poppers.

A gay German guy and his American lover ran a wonderful restaurant called Little Bavaria where my friends and I loved their schnitzel and gnocchi and sweet and sour red cabbage. I loved trying out all the restaurants, and not only the gay ones. At the Cazanoma Lodge, when you ordered the rainbow trout, a busboy would lead you outside and down the stairs to a pond and hand you a fishing pole to catch your own.

With so much good food in and all around Guerneville, The Woods never tried to be a fine dining destination again. The days of movie stars dressed in diamonds and furs with silver cigarette holders sharing bon mots at the elegant old Hexagon House were a mere memory.

The café perched across Fife Creek was the only place to eat if you were staying at The Woods if you didn't want to drive into town. It had a menu more like a diner than a fancy restaurant. I like to think of what they served as standard gay food, like what you might order at Orphan Andy's in the Castro or the Clover Grill on Bourbon Street in New Orleans, not that there's anything wrong with that kind of eating.

You could also get a Bloody Mary at the bar and take it with you to the café at The Woods. Sometimes steak and eggs with crispy hash browns and strong coffee is just the right cure for a hangover... as long as you don't forget the Bloody Mary.

CHAPTER EIGHTEEN:
My short-lived career as a columnist

Some guy named Fred Brothers got my number and called to ask if I was interested in writing a newspaper column. He was starting a new gay newspaper in San Francisco called *Castro Times* to compete with the *B.A.R.* and *The Sentinel* and *Coming Up!* I was not a well-known writer by any means, but I had been published in *Christopher Street* magazine out of New York and had published poetry and articles in lots of little quarterlies, reviews, and gay rags, none of it for very much money, if any. This guy wasn't offering any financial incentives either, but I thought about it for a few days and decided it might be fun.

His paper came out once a month and I still had never met the man when I started writing for him. We talked on the phone a couple of times and I typed up my column and sent it to him in an envelope in those days before email. After a couple of months he called to say that he was driving up from the city on a Saturday afternoon and would like to meet with me in person. He already had my address, but I gave him directions to find the big blue house with the statue of a donkey out in front. Then I almost forgot about him.

Saturdays were usually when Jon and Bobby and Bob were all there, in and out of the pool, passing joints, sunbathing, sometimes barbecuing and blending margaritas. This particular Saturday was no exception, plus we had a few extra guys there, maybe tricks from the night before. I didn't have to be at work until the evening, so I had plenty of time to spend with my weekend housemates.

So this publisher Fred shows up, a frumpy middle-aged guy wearing baggy clothes that were much too hot for the season. It was easy to see from the front door of the main house all the way through to the pool out in back. He must have already been salivating when I let him in and offered him a beer. We made our way to the back deck where I introduced him and he plopped down in a shady spot where he could watch the frolicking of half a dozen young gay guys wearing nothing but Speedos and SPF30. I don't remember that he and I had much of a "meeting" that day, but he was in no hurry to leave and hung around for a couple of hours .

I had been enjoying exploring the Russian River and writing about my weekday adventures, reviewing the places I discovered where I liked to eat, as well as filling my readers in on what was happening at the bars and discos. But a short time later Fred called to inform me that he had deleted my mention of a certain restaurant I mentioned because they hadn't bought an advertisement in his paper.

By the following month, he had a list for me of the businesses that did advertise in his rag and told me I needed to write glowingly about them in my column. No more coverage of Russian River events and no more notices about which entertainers were appearing live at The Woods that month unless they took out an ad. No more exploring the history of the region, either. Just advertising.

I lasted a couple more months and then I told him I didn't have time to write a column anymore. The season was in full swing. I wasn't burning any bridges behind me, but it wasn't as if this were a job that fulfilled me in any way.

One day I mentioned my old column to my fellow bartender Gabriel Starr. We had become good buddies by then, but didn't talk much about things outside of work, the customers, the bosses, and such. He said, "Wow… that was you? I guess I never knew your last name before!"

"Yeah, did you read my column?"

"I never missed it! My friend Kora (Danny Koralevsky— Gabriel had a nickname for everybody!) and I would always read it together and laugh and laugh. What a pile of crap! That whole paper is, but that column just got worse every month."

My jaw dropped and I stood there in shock for a moment as I realized he was absolutely right. I was so impressed with Gabe for telling me what he thought without mincing any words that our friendship only grew closer after that. I think he was impressed with me too because I agreed with him 100% and didn't bother to make any excuses. I told him about the creepy old guy wanting to have "meetings" by the pool at my house when a bunch of half-naked guys were all out there and we laughed about that too. I was just glad my newspaper column writing was in the past. I would find much better things to write books about in the future.

California

DATA-BOY

In Los Angeles: (213) 656-2960
In San Francisco: (415) 821-1244

AN ENTERTAINMENT MAGAZINE   ISSUE 324   APRIL 14, 1983

The Woods

WOODS

RUSSIAN RIVER RESORT

CHAPTER NINETEEN:
Bohemians

Guerneville had always felt to me like a sleepy little town where a tourist could buy suntan lotion and picture postcards of redwood trees and get a fishing license to go with their new rod and reel from King's Sport & Tackle. They might even stop in for an afternoon beer at the Rainbow Cattle Company, the most inviting saloon on the main drag, without even knowing they were in a gay bar.

One big exception to the small town feeling occurred every time Main Street was bumper to bumper with stretch limousines. They jammed River Road from the Santa Rosa turn-off all the way to Monte Rio when some of the richest and most conservative men in the world were on their way to Bohemian Grove for their annual two-week-long summer encampment.

If you are familiar with Armistead Maupin's *Tales of the City* series of books, you might remember that much of the plot of one of them, *Significant Others*, takes place in or near the grove. It is also the backdrop for the book, *Bohemian Grove: Cult of Conspiracy*, a documentary *Dark Secrets: Inside Bohemian Grove*, and a 2012 horror film called *The Conspiracy: 9/11, Illuminati, and the Bohemian Grove*.

The Grove covers nearly 3,000 acres of Douglas firs and 1,000-year-old redwoods with a man-made lake where the ritual known as the "Cremation of Care" takes place at the beginning of each encampment. Membership to the all-male club costs $25,000 plus annual fees for the privilege of letting loose in private in the great outdoors. Almost all of the Republican U.S. Presidents have been to the grove since its founding in 1878.

I found a videotape on the internet of President Richard Nixon talking about the Grove. I'm not sure if it was part of the infamous Watergate tapes, but on it he says, "The Bohemian Grove, that I attend from time to time, is the most faggy goddamn thing you can imagine… the San Francisco crowd that goes there… I won't even shake hands with anyone from San Francisco!"

I never realized before what a homophobe Nixon was, in addition to all his other character traits. If only he were alive a few decades later he might have encountered the annual gathering known as *Lazy Bear Weekend*, which now lasts a week, when about 3,000 gay, hairy, burly, and lazy revelers from around the world celebrate in Guerneville and other resort areas along the Russian River.

When I started working at The Woods, some of the waiters who had worked there in past years when it was still the elegant Hexagon House restaurant told me wonderful stories about the Bohemians. It was well-known that all of the rooms and cabins there were booked up every year at that time by some of the most beautiful and high-priced call girls from all over the world. The Bohemians would come for dinner and the ladies would make themselves available at one of the bars. Waiters told me about rich old white slobs inviting one or more of these gorgeous women to join them at their tables and setting hundred-dollar bills on fire from the candle on the table and then using the flaming money to light the ladies' cigarettes.

Obviously, not all of the Bohemians are as "goddamn faggy" as Richard Nixon believed. All of us who worked at The Woods that first season when it turned into a gay resort enjoyed watching the limousines come all the way up Armstrong Woods Road during that year's encampment. The men would step inside the front door expecting to see the old formal dining room drenched in candle-lit silver and crystal and crisp white linens. Instead of finding lovely ladies of the evening, they discovered sweaty, shirtless young men in cowboy boots or sneakers dancing with each other and snorting poppers under bright colored lights and a mirror ball.

They never made that mistake twice unless they were gay, but in that case, they wouldn't have gone there looking for women for sex.

Al, one of the owners, told me that he'd gotten to be friends with some of the girls over the years and a few of them did stop by in the afternoons to have a drink and say hello to some of the old staff they had known in past years. They had all moved to Northwood Lodge this year and it was even more convenient for everyone, located just up the road from the main entrance to Bohemian Grove.

One of the girls I'll call Elena invited Al and me over to Northwood for a visit one afternoon, so the two of us got in his car and went. We found Elena's cottage and she showed us her closet filled with the most amazing collection of designer gowns I've ever seen outside of Donna Sachet's house when she lived on Castro Street. Every drag queen I know would have gasped!

Elena then showed us pictures of her handsome son, maybe ten years old, at his private boarding school in Switzerland. He was back home in Argentina for the summer and she was very proud of him. I was surprised that she was Argentinean because her English was so perfect I thought she was from the USA. When I mentioned that, she told me, "I grew up living all over the world. I'm quite fluent in several languages."

She said she was sorry she didn't have anything to offer us to drink, but we were only steps away from the bar at the lodge so she invited us there, "But first..." she said, "a little treat?" Elena pulled out a mirror, set it on the coffee table, and dumped out the contents of a small brown bottle and chopped a couple of big fat lines of cocaine for each of us.

Dinner at the Bohemian Grove

At the bar, Al recognized a couple of the girls he knew from past years at the Hexagon House, so the three of us joined their large round table and Al ordered a round of drinks for everyone. It was only mid-afternoon, but the place was busy, mostly with beautiful women. At one point Elena looked across the room and caught the eye of a rugged looking man, maybe in his early fifties, wearing a yellow knit shirt over the start of a pot-belly, blue polyester slacks, and a wide white belt to match his loafers, gold chains on his neck and one wrist and a huge gold watch on the other.

Elena excused herself from our table and we watched the man follow her outside a minute later. Not too faggy at all!

When Elena came back to join us she sat down, touched up her lipstick, and waved a hundred dollar bill at the cocktail waitress to order another round of drinks for our table. She was much too smart to burn them.

CHAPTER TWENTY:
More divas

Linda Hopkins was so full of love she was radiant and it was a total joy for me to get to know her. She announced at the start of her performance that she liked Budweiser, so people in the audience kept buying beers and sending them up to her with the cocktail waiters. She poured each long-necked brown bottle into a tall chilled glass that she lifted to her lips and drank all down at once. I won't say she was drunk, but about halfway through her show she slipped and fell and banged up her knee badly enough that she needed to sit down for a while.

Another wonderful singer, Napata Mero, was in the audience that night and Linda asked her if she'd come up and do a number while Linda rested. Napata sang "Since I Fell for You" and by the time she finished, to great applause, Linda was ready to get back up and go on with her show.

Afterward, Linda Hopkins and I sat down and played Ms. Pacman together. It was one of those video games where the screen was built into the top of a table so we sat on either side facing each other. She kept on drinking beers and I had more scotch. I only drank scotch on cabaret nights. It seemed to fit the atmosphere of sitting back and listening to a soulful singer in a smoky room.

Most of the entertainers who performed at The Woods stayed in room #20 on the ground floor of the L-shaped hotel building, just a few yards across the driveway from the stage door, that led them through the former kitchen of the fabulous old Hexagon House Restaurant. Room #20 was at the end of the small side of the L and could open into room #21 next door if the performer had an accompanist or manager or hairdresser or whomever. The L wrapped around an old kidney shaped swimming pool. My fellow bartender Gabriel Starr called it *The Flintstones* pool, but I'm not even sure why anymore. I guess it reminded him of both 1940s suburbia and caveman times. The other pool, the newer, bigger one out back between the cabins was the clothing-optional one.

The Flintstones Pool

When it was finally time for Linda Hopkins to go to bed, I walked her back to room #20 and she asked me to come in and help her get undressed. Under her dress she was wearing a corset that she needed help to undo all the little hooks and eyes down the back. I didn't think to ask her how she had gotten it on in the first place. I quickly said good-night and got out of there. As much as I liked her, I didn't care to see any more of Linda Hopkins than I already had.

A few years later, in 1989, she co-starred with Ruth Brown in *Black and Blue on Broadway*, which Robert Altman later recorded as a film. Both singers received Tony Award nominations for Leading Actress in a Musical, coincidentally the same year Sharon McNight was nominated for *Starmites*. Ruth Brown won.

The next day, the afternoon after Linda Hopkins performance at The Woods, I went horseback riding with Napata Mero and her handsome husband. Some smart entrepreneur that summer had set up a business offering rides from The Woods through the redwood forest and up to an old abandoned silver mine. I'm sure that was the last time I was ever on horseback.

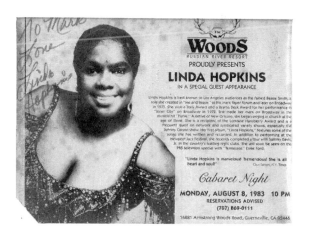

Wayland Flowers never performed at The Woods while I was working there, but he came around at least a couple of times.

When the place wasn't busy he would sit at the bar and bring out his hilarious puppet "Madame" and let her hold court. It was even better than seeing him on stage because Madame could be as outrageous as she wanted. Wayland never bothered to learn how to "throw his voice," so you could always see his lips moving. In Madame's many television appearances (she even had her own sitcom for a while) the cameraman could easily focus on her without him. In person, Madame often pointed to Wayland and said, "He's no ventriloquist…and I'm no fuckin' dummy!" Peter Marshall was the original host of the long-running game show *Hollywood Squares,* about whom Madame cracked, "Peter Marshall…sounds like the security guard at a gay bar!" Talking about her dear friend Maude, Madame said, "Maude's not too bright, you know. I bought her a vibrator for Christmas. She knocked out three teeth the first day!"

At the height of the tourist season The Woods featured a live performer almost every Saturday night on the stage above the dance floor. It was there on the dance floor under the spinning mirror ball that the magic happened, the almost tribal ritual of moving to the music while surrounded by dozens of half-naked men. I remember times when Chris Osborne was the manager, he would get a few bottles of poppers (we had them for sale at the coat check), throw away the lids and pass them out to people at the edges of the dance floor with the instructions to "pass them on!" By about midnight the crowd was usually high enough to bring a disco diva out onto the stage. Nearly every one-hit disco wonder performed at the place and there were others like Sylvester who were true disco stars. He performed at The Woods too many times for me to count.

I can't remember all the singers' names or songs, but Scherrie Payne had a hit with "I'm Gonna Let My Heart Do The Walking."

She was Freda Payne's younger sister and performed as one of the Supremes from '73–'77.

Magda Layna had a hit with her Hi-NRG/Disco version of the Three Degrees' "When Will I See You Again?" released by Megatone Records, which was founded in San Francisco by legendary dance music composer and recording artist Patrick Cowley. Megatone was the label for most of Sylvester's music as well as Frank Loverde (or just Loverde) whose hits were "Die Hard Lover" and "My World Is Empty Without You" as well as Paul Parker's "Right on Target" who was pure beefcake, not to be confused with my porn star friend Al Parker.

Viola Wills and I had the connection of both being from Minnesota. Earlier in her career, she had sung with Barry White and The Love Unlimited Orchestra and toured as a background vocalist for Joe Cocker. For several years after I moved back to the San Francisco, she was the closing act at the Folsom Street Fair. Each year I would find her trailer backstage for hugs and a visit before she went out to perform her hits like "Gonna Get Along Without You Now" and a disco version of "If You Could Read My Mind"—I adored her.

Marlena Shaw performed at The Woods one night. She had hits with "Go Away Little Boy" and a disco cover of Diana Ross' longest-charting pop record, "Touch Me in the Morning."

Back in 1975, on my first ever trip to Oakland's fabulous Art Deco palace, The Paramount Theater, I got to see LaBelle perform their huge hit "Lady Marmalade." Patti LaBelle never performed at The Woods, but the other two members of the trio did. Sarah Dash had a solo hit with "Sinner Man" and Nona Hendryx had songs such as "Messin' With My Mind" and "Do What You Wanna Do."

Gwen Jonae performed "Red Light Lover" and "Destiny" at The Woods. Angela Clemmons did "Give Me Just a Little More Time" and Anita Ward had a hit with "Ring My Bell."

SUMMER SEASON 1982

OUR PREMIER EVENT:

MEMORIAL DAY WEEKEND

THE PATRICK COWLEY SINGERS
performing Menergy, Megatron Man and I Wanna Take You Home

MUSIC • PAUL DOUGAN   LIGHTS • STEVE MART   SET DESIGN • LUMINSIONS   SOUND • TRONDSON
SATURDAY MAY 29 AND SUNDAY MAY 30 DANCE HALL STAGE 9 PM -4 AM COVER $6.00

ALSO THE SAME WEEKEND:

FRIDAY MAY 28 — LEGENDS - The first showing of a touring exhibition of fine pencil illustrations by artist William Moore displayed in the dance hall 3 -8 pm.

SUNDAY MAY 30 — A sunny tea dance featuring a guest d.j. and complimented by our new patio bar.

MONDAY MAY 31 — Local's Night returns with some new surprises.

COMING EVENTS

JUNE 12 - 14 — A new theme from the designers who last year brought you the Black Forest, Moon River, White Forest and New Year's Eve parties.

FOURTH OF JULY — A multi-media celebration of the red, white and blue.

AUGUST 12 - 14 — "Tropical Forest" features the warmth of Polynesia with its flowers, luaus, volcanoes and entertainment.

LABOR DAY — SYLVESTER'S BIRTHDAY PARTY!

AND MORE EVENTS TO BE ANNOUNCED

WOOD S CAFE
Recently refurbished and a new menu for your dining pleasure.
LODGING AND DAY-USE FACILITIES AVAILABLE
16881 Armstrong Woods Road, Guerneville, Ca. 95446 (707) 869-0111

CHAPTER TWENTY ONE:
Patty, Jane Dornacker, Gail Wilson, and the first Mister Northern California Drummer Contest

It must have been my second season at the Russian River when The Woods got a new general manager named Patty. Chris Osborne, the first season's manager, moved back to the city and we remained friends for years. Patty was a Russian River local, a lipstick lesbian who shared a home with her partner Joy and their children from previous relationships. It was not unusual in those days for gay men to get married and have children before they came out and it seemed an even more ordinary experience among gay women.

It was common knowledge that one of Patty's children was fathered by Elvis Presley. I never asked her about it to her face and I can't remember who told me—probably Gabriel—but I heard there had also been a big story in one of the tabloids a while back about Elvis' "love child" living in northern California. It said that as a teenager, Patty was a huge Elvis fan who finagled a way backstage after one of his concerts and threw herself at him. Nine months later Patty had a baby boy who came out swiveling his hips.

To be honest, I only saw Patty and Joy's kids once or twice and I couldn't tell which of them belonged to whom. From my perspective, they were just a pack of noisy little monsters and none of them made me stop and think, "Wow, he's the spitting image of Elvis!"

I liked Patty okay, but I was never quite sure of what her job was. I suppose she counted the bartenders' banks and kept track of inventory, ordered liquor and lemons and limes, cocktail onions and serviettes. I remember that she smoked a lot, but we all smoked cigarettes in those days. They were cheap and we were young and foolish.

Patty always carried a huge ring of keys that jangled so loudly she could never sneak up on you. She also carried a pack of smokes in a worn leather cigarette case and a cheap plastic lighter. I remember how she pranced around with her elbows bent at her sides at a 90-degree angle so that both forearms were in front of her with her hands bent at the wrist so that her perfectly polished fingernails pointed toward the floor. I don't know how she managed that while carrying so much stuff, but that's how I remember her.

Patty took her position very seriously. I think it was Alexander Pope who said, "A little knowledge can be a dangerous thing." In Patty's case, a little power could be too. She loved being the boss of so many young gay men and she let us know it, while at the same time she was so desperate to be loved by one and all that she tried to behave like a benevolent ruler. She seemed to expect that any praise from her should be met with groveling thanks. Looking back, the whole dynamic of Patty as boss seems incredibly silly, but we were all stoned half the time anyway, so we just tried to get along.

⌐∽

I had been a music major when I started college and then took a lot of theater courses when I was working at the Children's Theatre in Minneapolis. I was mainly there for my ability to play the saxophone, but I paid close attention to how everything worked in the live theater. I learned a lot from the vantage point of the orchestra pit and from hanging out with my actor/singer/dancer friends backstage and elsewhere.

While I lived in San Francisco before the river move, I had worked in restaurants, but also helped my first serious boyfriend Armando get his highly successful catering business up and running. I learned a lot from him too, including how to bartend, plus a lot about food and all about how to throw a party.

During the winter at the river, business slows way down, so I thought I might be able to use my theater and catering backgrounds to rustle up some business in the off-season. The redwoods were still beautiful in the winter, after all, especially with the smell of rain on the forests and wood-burning stoves and fireplaces permeating the air in that whole part of the state.

Before I eventually moved back to the city, I created the aforementioned Mister Russian River contest and the annual bartenders' bash, inviting gay bartenders and bar backs and bar owners from not only San Francisco, but also every gay bar in northern California, including Sacramento, San Jose, Santa Rosa, and Guerneville, of course. I started the annual Leather Weekend at The Woods and produced the Mister Northern California Drummer contest in conjunction with John Embry, publisher of *Drummer Magazine*. The first year they sent one of their employees, Karl Stewart, to produce it with me and the following years I did it on my own.

I'm not sure how many times The Woods hosted the Drummer contest. It was over thirty years ago, but through the power of social media, I've been able to reach two of the winners, John Ponce (1982) who is living in Palm Springs now, as are so many of the relatively few survivors of the era, and Sonny Cline (1984) in New Jersey. The Mister Drummer contest was the most work of any of the events I did. I had to line up all the judges, handle the advertising, convince bars and resorts to sponsor contestants to represent them, and it often fell to me to find good looking guys who liked to show off. The hot guys were the easiest part, actually.

One year Patty insisted that I should be the contestant representing The Woods. I thought about it. I tried to imagine myself dressed in all my leather on the stage above the dance floor. I could more easily see myself wearing just a Speedo during the physique competition which I always held outdoors on Saturday afternoon beside the clothing-optional pool. I was in pretty good shape. I had joined the Guerneville gym. I had been naked at the nude pool lots of times, although I usually wore a swim suit for the sake of getting a tan line.

Patty was much more excited about my being in the contest than I was. The closer the time came to make a decision, the more I dreaded it. It felt like looking forward to having some painful surgery. Besides, I was too busy putting the whole weekend together. Wouldn't it be unethical for someone who was running the contest to be *in* the contest? What if I won? It would look fixed. Patty was disappointed, but I finally had to flat-out refuse and she got over it.

I had lined up guys from all the major resorts and from some of the most popular gay bars in San Francisco. I already knew some of them and most of them were really nice guys, many of whom became my friends, if not tricks. I was just glad I wasn't competing with any of them. Carl, Gene, and Al, the owners of The Woods, still wanted a contestant, though, so they ended up hiring a model they flew up from Hollywood, all expenses paid.

I had seen his nude pictures on calendars and greeting cards and in magazines like *Honcho* and *Blueboy* and *Inches*, but he wasn't really the *Drummer* type. He was stunning in photographs, with his chiseled features, an amazing face from any angle, a perfect body, sculpted like marble, a huge dick, and all the charm and personality of a raw rutabaga. In person, all of that charisma of the camera quickly melted away.

The rest of the contestants always developed a genial camaraderie over the course of the three days of the contest, but not the guy from L.A. The owners of The Woods thought he was a shoe-in to win the sash, but I think he came in third or fourth. I can't say that I was disappointed.

Jane Dornacker performed at The Woods one Monday night for a "Locals' Night" that was advertised as "Comedy Night at The Woods." Three comics performed that evening, but Jane was saved for last and she's the only one I remember. That night was the first time I ever met Jane in person and I fell in love with her right away. How could anyone not fall in love with Jane Dornacker? I first met the wonderful Marga Gomez at The Woods too, but she performed there another time.

That night at The Woods wasn't the first time I had seen Jane perform, however. That must have been when Market Street was torn up to build the MUNI metro subway system. The Castro Street station entrance was covered over with plywood for months. It was where Harvey Milk gathered big crowds with his bullhorn to lead us to march to City Hall and that was where Jane somehow managed to get a microphone, speakers, and an electronic piano keyboard on top so that she could entertain the bar crowds on weekend nights, sometimes even long after the bars closed at 2 a.m.

Jane would soon perform at comedy clubs around the city, especially at the legendary Valencia Rose, along with Whoopi Goldberg, Lea Delaria, and Tom Ammiano. Jane did a two-woman show with Whoopi Goldberg at the Victoria Theater, also in the heart of San Francisco's Mission District, at a time when Jane was probably better known than Whoopi was.

Jane was over six feet tall and gorgeous, plus she always wore high heels and often swept up her thick mane of dark red hair and piled it on top of her head, especially when she did her character Marge Battaglia. Jane must have loosely based Marge on Julia Child because she used similar speech patterns, but Marge was not a chef. She was a "snackologist" who discussed the importance of mucous in one's diet, the long shelf-life of Hostess Sno-Balls, and demonstrated how they could be taken apart and the top used as a condom with the coconut icing acting as a French tickler. Marge was also a housewife who always mentioned needing to get back home to her husband Bill and the kids who were probably waiting up for her in Snackramento.

Jane and I became great friends over the next few years until her untimely on-air death in a helicopter crash in NY's Hudson River in 1986. I used to call her my "Amazon friend" because she was so hugely beautiful. This was when the word Amazon referred to the mythological female Greek warriors, more than a decade before Jeff Bezos founded the company that is slowly devouring the world of retail as we once knew it. During Jane's day-job as a "trafficologist" she reported on the morning commute and made it funny. She would talk to her daughter Naomi at home over the radio and tell her to get up and go to school. I remember her announcing a car crash as "a vehicular flambé on the Golden Gate Bridge. Apparently someone has lost control of the master/subordinate relationship between driver and automobile." I can still picture Jane bopping around town and sometimes arriving at a comedy gig in a little three-wheeled vehicle with open sides and a roof. It might have been invented for postal workers to deliver mail, but I think Jane's belonged to KFRC, a local San Francisco radio station. When Jane arrived somewhere in her vehicle, she didn't just step out of it like a normal person climbs out of a car. She *emerged* with her big hair and her big tits and a big smile and an even bigger personality.

On stage, Jane combined songs and story-telling. She once told me she had played the piano at the very first Haight Street Fair to accompany her daughter Naomi and a group of her little girlfriends when they sang a number on the main stage at Haight and Masonic. Jane performed with and co-wrote songs for The Tubes, a San Francisco-based rock band, most notably "Don't Touch Me There" from their 1976 album, *Young and Rich*.

Jane had also performed as the lead singer Leila with the group Leila and the Snakes doing such memorable hits as "Rock-n-Roll Weirdos." I saw her in that character of Leila at The Palms on Polk Street when the Polk Gulch neighborhood was the center of gay life in San Francisco, even before the Castro. My dear friend (and birthday-mate, along with Al Parker) Rita Rockett was a cocktail waitress at The Palms before I knew either of them. Rita probably saw Jane, as Leila, perform there before I did. Sylvester sang at The Palms too and he and Rita became great friends. In the late '70s, San Francisco felt like such a small town that everyone knew everyone else, or at least knew someone who did.

I remember that night when Jane performed at The Woods was the first time I heard her tell her famous dick joke. Actually, what she said was, "I don't tell jokes. I'm not that kind of comedienne, but sometimes I feel that it's sort of like part of my job to report them, so here goes: 'What is white and ten inches long? (long pause) Nothing!'"

As badly as it exploited stereotypes, that one always got a big laugh, especially with a gay audience. What was funny to me was when I later discovered that Jane was speaking from her own experience. When I finally moved back to the city from the Russian River and Jane had moved on to New York, she would stay with me sometimes when she was back in town, especially when I booked her to perform somewhere locally. I lived south of Market on Shotwell Street and Jane and I made a deal that whichever one of us brought home a date first got to have the bed and the other one got the couch. Jane always beat me home and I never knew Jane to bring home any guys who weren't black and absolutely gorgeous! I only pretended to be asleep on the couch while I watched them go back and forth to the bathroom naked.

Jane Dornaker's fame grew a lot when she appeared as Nurse Murch in Philip Kaufman's movie adaptation of Tom Wolfe's non-fiction novel *The Right Stuff* which chronicles the first 15 years of America's space program.

Jane was always so much fun to run around with or to just hang out. I picked her up in my pickup truck many times at her apartment in the Haight where she and Naomi lived on Central Avenue, across the street from Buena Vista Park. When she and I took the train for her to perform at an event I booked for her at a gay bar in San Jose, she entertained everyone on our car, just by being herself. No one was a stranger to Jane Dornacker. She treated everyone like a good friend.

The first year we held the Mister Northern California Drummer Contest at The Woods, we booked Jane to do a dinner show on Friday night, which would end just before the dance floor opened. She was supposed to bring out and introduce all the contestants for that year's contest and have some fun with them as part of her act. Jane was terrific at being spontaneous with hysterically funny ad libs.

Unfortunately, something came up that made it impossible for Jane to be there. Maybe she was sick (or hungover) but we had to find a replacement in short order. I looked through that week's most recent gay newspapers from the city. There were the *Bay Area Reporter*, *The Sentinel*, *The Voice*, and maybe one or two other ones at the time. I don't think the *Bay Times* had started yet, but nearly all of the recent papers had ads or articles or reviews about a cabaret singer named Gail Wilson. Her picture was even on the cover of one of them in her magenta hair and faux-leopard coat. Someone knew someone who knew Gail and it turned out she was available that night and so was her piano accompanist.

Gail was a singer, not a comedienne, but parts of her act were very funny. She did a hilarious medley of songs as Karen Carpenter that was a standard part of her show right up until Karen Carpenter died of anorexia (officially congestive heart failure) in 1983 and Gail had to shelve it for a few years.

Gail also did a Connie Francis medley, which was a little kinder to its subject, but still very entertaining. It ended with Gail belting out "Where the Boys Are" like a hymn or an anthem and at that moment the contestants for that year's Mister Northern California Drummer joined Gail onstage. As it turned out, Gail was probably a better choice for that gig, anyway. Jane often ended her show with a song about her walking down Polk Street and being mistaken for a drag queen. She always encouraged the audience to sing along, belting out "Drag Queen! Drag Queen! Drag Queen!" which would not have been at all appropriate for a leather title contest.

Gail Wilson and I became great friends too, over the next several years, and still are, but she swears she doesn't remember me from that night at The Woods. I guess that's what friends are for sometimes... to keep us humble.

DONALD McLEAN'S
ENTERTAINMENT SCENE

CABARET: GAIL WILSON

GAIL WILSON — A dazzling new singer makes a dynamic debut on the local cabaret scene.

GAIL WILSON, of the flaming iodine hair and bubbling personality, is hardly a newcomer in any sense. For the past four years she has been one-third of the hit vocal trio Swing in L.A. Now she's back in San Francisco on her own and if I had to make a bet who will be the big San Francisco discovery of '82, my money's on the redhead.

First of all, like all smart performers, she's surrounded herself with topnotch people—she has James Dunk backing her up on piano and vocally, so her act is a duet of talent. She also has Jeff Schmidt, who writes wonderful special material that bolsters her act in no small degree; he is responsible for a brilliantly scathing song parody of The Carpenters, using their own hits against them. It brought down the house with laughter and applause. These gifted gentlemen would be working in vain of course, unless the center of the picture delivers. Fear not, this Wilson gal can do it all equally well; her act, after only two months locally, would play just as well in the Venetian Room as Our Kitchen. Problems are minor — The Carpenter medley should be placed earlier on, because it's almost impossible to top for a big finish, an arrangement of "Sweet Georgia Brown" is a throwaway, not a closer.. . and that's about the only negative there is to find.

She works the room and her audience with a gracious ease and humor that instantly makes everyone relax, knowing they're in the hands of a very secure professional. She sings the same way — no strain, no forced personality, no dramtic "big" tremulous finish, just solid vocal ease, whether caressing a smoky, "I Never Thought I'd Break" by Peter Allen, ripping through a jazz rendition of "You Can Depend On Me" that turns the song inside out, or paying homage to the late Nat King Cole with a medley of his uptempo hits. She slides into a sneakily seductive "Peel Me A Grape" by saying — "There are two kinds of daddies in this world. The first kind buys you a tricycle; the other kind buys you a Thunderbird!"

With lines like this, and with impeccable delivery, musical arrangements that are always interesting and unique, plus showmanship that's upbeat without being brassy, GAIL WILSON would seem destined to be the logical successor for the same devoted audience that discovered Sharon McNight a few years back. This is a major talent headed for the top of the "local singing ladies" vocal heap.

The Voice, March 12, 1982

CHAPTER TWENTY TWO:
Lesbians

Patty, The Woods' manager, and her partner Joy were some of the first "out" lesbians I ever knew. Well, I'd met famous gay political women like Barbara Giddings through John Preston back in the days when we lived in Minneapolis, but an evening at dinner was different from daily exposure. Since Patty and Joy both had children from previous relationships with men—Elvis and/or others—they seemed a bit more motherly than dyke-ish to me. Joy was pretty butch compared to Patty, but then, even the nelliest of gay guys was pretty butch compared to Patty.

There was a time in history when gay men and lesbians lived in two very different worlds. We had our bars and they had theirs. I would never say that I hated lesbians, but there were lots of hard-core man-hating dykes living in Sonoma County in those days and I was sort of scared of them. They'd come out to the Russian River bars on weekends, mostly, and get drunk and act out their hostility toward anyone without a vagina. I remember sitting at the bar at Fife's one afternoon, having a cold beer, minding my own business, when a dyke five stools down from me accused me of knocking her cowboy hat on the floor. She had had it perched on the bar stool beside her with her back turned to me, so she probably bumped it herself. I couldn't have reached it if I'd wanted to, but she was looking for a fight.

I finished my beer and got up and left and she finally went back to talking with the bartender who seemed to be a friend (or girlfriend) of hers. Fife's hired a mix of male and female bar staff, unlike The Woods. We weren't that politically correct on the north side of town.

Whenever I was behind the bar at The Woods, I secretly cringed when I saw those country dykes approach the bar. They would order the weirdest drinks that took a lot of time to make when I was already busy and they never tipped.

Oldest lesbian joke in the world:
Q: What's the difference between a lesbian and a canoe?
A: Canoes tip!

Or they would order a bottle of Calistoga water and keep refilling it all night with tap water from the restroom sinks. I heard that some bars fixed their restroom sinks so that they only put out warm water in order to discourage patrons from doing that. The housekeeping crew at The Woods would always find empty pint liquor bottles in the women's restroom that had been snuck in past the doorman.

We were there to sell drinks. That was where most of the money came from to pay the disc jockey and the light man and the gardeners and the maids, all the staff that most people scarcely noticed unless they had a complaint about something.

One Saturday night a tough country dyke came up to my bar and ordered a cup of coffee with heavy cream and lots of sugar. I poured it and set it on the bar, "That'll be one dollar, please." That was the minimum charge at the bar if you wanted a glass of 7-Up or a Coke or coffee or tap water on ice, it was all a dollar.

She took one sip and said it needed more sugar. Then more cream. I got it for her and repeated, "One dollar, please."

She said something like, "Alright, alright, asshole. Hang on a damn minute and you'll get your fuckin' dollar!" She reached inside the pockets of her bib overalls and finally came up with one hundred lint-covered pennies. She counted them out in rows of ten on the bar while I was slinging drinks as fast as I could to the guys who had been waiting behind her and were now reaching around her as best they could.

When she finally got the hundred pennies lined up, I picked up the nearest trash can, held it to the lip of the bar, and swept all the pennies into it. You should have seen the look on her face. "What the fuck? What'd you do that for? That was a dollar's worth of pennies!"

"So that you won't try to pull that stunt on another bartender tonight. Now move! You're blocking my service station. Get out of the way and no free refills!"

My fear of butch lesbians gradually subsided, but not until I eventually moved back to the city. Even then it took a while. There was a lesbian bar in the Castro called Francine's on the corner of 18TH and Collingwood, where The Edge has been in business ever since Francine sold her bar.

Francine was a rare piece of work! She was a transwoman with large saggy breasts and a huge penis that she was still very proud of. She hobbled around as bow-legged as could be in short skirts and spiky high heels that were crying for mercy. Francine was cheap. And rich! It was said that she drove to Detroit every year to trade in her Corvette for the newest model because she could avoid some kind of taxes or fees that way. I never understood it.

Francine never tipped and she didn't spend any money trying to look good, either. No wigs, no heavy make-up, she simply tied her few strands of hair into a thin pony tail at the back of her head.

Francine owned several bars in her day and I heard she was planning to open one at the Russian River, had it not been for an arrest warrant that made her ineligible to obtain a liquor license in Sonoma County. The story goes that she was drinking in the Rainbow Cattle Company and stepped outside the back door to take a leak in the alley. She lifted her skirt just as a police car came by and caught her huge schlong in its search lights, resulting in a charge of indecent exposure. People laughed that she could have been charged with indecent exposure anytime she appeared in public.

One afternoon I went into Francine's bar in the Castro with a lesbian couple I knew. We sat down on three barstools with me in the middle and ordered our drinks. The very butch bartender proceeded to make two drinks that she placed in front of the two women, who said, "What about Mark's drink? He's our friend."

The bartender said, "I don't see anyone else here."

They left their full drinks on the bar without paying for them and we all walked across the street to the Pendulum where we got served with no problem. The Pendulum was then known as a "black men's bar" but they were happy to serve just about anyone who had money and didn't cause problems.

There used to be several lesbian bars in San Francisco. One was called Peg's Place. I googled it and here are the highlights of its history:

Peg's Place was located at 4737 Geary Boulevard, described as a "sedate location for gay women to socialize", featuring "unprepossessing décor, a fake gas fed fireplace, pool and a Pong machine." An ex-patron, interviewed in 2015, said the bar in its early days was a place where "you could wear pants, but not blue jeans.... "I think they wanted you to be--maybe they call it classy. They didn't want to think they catered to bums or truck-driver types."

On March 31, 1979, a group of ten to fifteen men, including some off-duty members of the San Francisco vice squad, were out celebrating a bachelor party. When they arrived at Peg's Place, the doorwoman denied them admission because they were carrying beer and were intoxicated. Some of the men reportedly yelled "Let's get the dykes" as they pushed their way into the bar. One of the men put the doorwoman in a chokehold; another beat the female bar owner with a pool cue. When the women said they were calling the cops, one of the men said, "We are the cops, and we'll do as we damn well please."

I remember a tiny lesbian bar on Sanchez just south of Duboce Park called Scott's Pit. I went there once with a straight woman I knew from work. She was pretty and friendly, so the other customers tolerated me being in their space. It felt like we were in someone's basement recreation room with a pool table in the middle. I think it had a garage door onto the street that they could open whenever they wanted to hose the place out.

Rikki Streicher owned both Maud's and Amelia's. I adored Rikki from the first time I met her. What a tiny but powerful woman! She once loaned me thousands of dollars to throw a dance party on a pier. She told me one time about being with a group of gay businessmen who were organizing a club for gay men who were millionaires. Rikki asked why they only wanted to include men and one of them laughed and said, "We never considered that there might be any lesbian millionaires."

Rikki told them, "Well, you're looking at one and I know several others." I don't know whether or not Rikki ever joined their club. I rather doubt it. She didn't need advice from them on running a business and she was already busy running two bars and a restaurant on Pier 50 and at least part ownership in a liquor store or two.

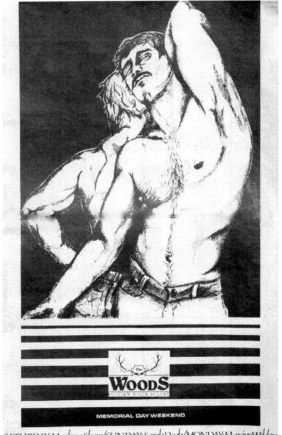

SATURDAY: Marlena Sham/SUNDAY: Sandy Daily/MONDAY: Maxine Weldon

All of those old lesbian bars are gone now, even the Lexington Club in the Mission district, which I never even set foot inside, but it seemed nice. The Wildside West in Bernal Heights is considered a women's bar, I guess, but they've never balked at serving me the few times I've been there. Some theorize that lesbians tend to pair off more readily than gay men do.

Second oldest lesbian joke in the world:

Q: What do lesbians bring on their second date?

A: A U-Haul

It may be true of several lesbians I have known that they are in long-term committed relationships, but they still like to go out for a drink now and then and see friends, so they go to bars where everyone is welcome.

When AIDS struck, lots of lesbians became our heroines. They could donate blood. They could care for the sick. Now I am getting ahead of myself in the story, but only to say that in time we learned to support one another, young and old, male and female and transgender and non-conforming, drag queens and leathermen who are sometimes one and the same.

The generation before mine fought an enormous battle for basic human rights. It only makes sense that all corners of the gay/queer community should band together whenever something threatens even one part of us.

CHAPTER TWENTY THREE:
Hot summer days and Greg Cowden

Midsummer days at the Russian River were as hot as my summer childhood days on the Minnesota farm where I grew up. So were midsummer nights, but I always preferred being too hot to being too cold. At least at the river there were swimming pools everywhere. It seemed like I only worked at The Woods on the weekends, but I know that one season I worked the new outdoor bar between the clothing-optional pool and the little café building that straddled Fife Creek. You could walk in the front door on the east side of the creek and walk out the back door on the west. It was cozy, with just a few tables and stools at the counter where you could watch the cook making your breakfast, lunch, or dinner.

The new pool bar had four blenders, one for pina coladas, one for banana daiquiris, one for strawberry daiquiris and the fourth one I used for the day's special, which was often margaritas. When the wild blackberries growing along the creek were at their juiciest ripeness, I would give a customer a paper cup and have them pick their own. When they brought them back to me I'd make them a fresh blackberry daiquiri and they loved it!

On weekends there must have been more then one cocktail waiter, with the "day-use" customers added to the mix of hotel and cabin guests as well as Woods employees and their friends. When I worked those Thursday afternoons I just had one cocktail waiter making trips around the two pools, one at a time, placing orders with me from the nude pool and then coming back with orders from the Flintstone's pool and picking up the drinks for the nude pool customers. I can't remember his name, but I want to call him Dick. Maybe it was because he had a huge one.

Dick always wore a loin cloth like Tarzan's to work the pools. It was just a waistband and two small triangles of soft smooth leather, like chamois, a little longer in the front than in the back, where most of his steely buns were exposed. In the front, it was just long enough to cover the head of his penis, which flopped around when he walked among the deck chairs and fell out entirely when he bent down to deliver drink orders. Dick made great tips and it was a lot of fun to work with him.

Tuesdays and Wednesdays I hardly ever worked. I loved to get in my truck and go exploring, looking for places along the river where gay men cruised. Sometimes I went exploring with a friend or a trick or with a trick who had become a friend. We would drive to the top of Armstrong Woods or rent scooters and go to the little hamburger place just west of Guerneville. It was little more than a shack, painted yellow, and they grilled hamburgers the size of salad plates on a big smoking grill served on yeasty buns big enough to hold them. They must have had a deal with the local bakery because I've never seen buns that huge in any store. They were delicious!

Sometimes we would stop at fruit stands that lined the back roads of Sonoma County. Cherries were my favorite thing to eat there or maybe the stone fruits when they were in perfect season, nectarines, apricots, plums and peaches.

One time Paul Cowden's brother Greg came to visit me. Greg worked with his big brother Paul at Cowden Automotive on Folsom Street in the city, where I always took my truck for service. All my friends and I lusted after Paul, but he was happily married to some guy. His little brother Greg was available though, and he turned out to be not so little after all, if you catch my drift.

Once Greg got out from under the shadow of his handsome older brother, he was a lot of fun and it turned out, he finally confessed, that he'd had the hots for me for a long time. It must have been a Tuesday morning when he drove up in his little Citroen Deux-Chevaux. It was the cutest car I'd ever seen and Greg knew how to fix anything that went wrong with it. He already had the top down, so as soon as he dropped off his bags, used my bathroom, and set up his little pup tent in my back yard, we got back in the car and went for a drive.

We crossed Wohler Bridge and headed north, if I'm not mistaken, north and east for many miles, we eventually passed the mansion at Spring Mountain Vineyard that was the setting for the '80s TV drama *Falcon Crest*. The further we got from the ocean the hotter the day grew to be. Greg had an ice chest wedged in behind our seats where he'd already chilled a couple of bottles of white wine. We bought more that day when we stopped at a couple of vineyards and at some point we pulled over to the side of the road and opened one. He'd brought real wine glasses too—no paper or plastic cups for us—and we savored the crisp fermented juices of the grapes that surrounded us. Then we smoked a joint and peeled off our t-shirts. It was way too hot for them, for sure.

I remember that we saw some geysers that day. They were nothing like Yellowstone Park, but still I had to admit that it was amazing to consider what goes on beneath the surface of this world that seems so solid. We too often take the earth for granted, especially in Califonia, until the next earthquake wakes us up from our complacency.

Greg and I also came across an old bottling plant out in the forest. The building had mostly crumbled and the ground was covered with hundreds of old soda bottles, many of them half-buried in the dirt and overgrown with weeds. We brought a few of them back to the blue house on Orchard Avenue and cleaned them up. They were clear or green glass bottles with raised lettering on the side, with names of brands of sodas I'd never even heard of, along with some old Coca-Cola bottles too. We didn't take home any of those, thinking they were too common. They might have been worth money to a collector today.

What I remember best about that trip with Greg was when we were headed back to my place. The temperature had to have been in the 90s and we were both drenched with sweat. Greg pulled over to a shady spot by the side of the road again and opened another bottle of wine. Once he got it open, he handed me the corkscrew to put it back in the glove compartment. When our fingers touched, we dropped the corkscrew on the floor of the car and finally went at each other! Deep kisses, sweaty arms and chests and faces, grinding as much of our bodies together as we could within the confines of that little car, standing up to do so, sweat flying everywhere, both our dicks pulled out of our pants and rock hard, poking at each other.

We heard a car coming so we quickly sat back down, tried to look innocent, and burst out laughing. We howled! Then we drove back to Guerneville and back to Orchard Avenue—fast—for a quick dip in the pool and then directly to my bed. I think Greg stayed with me two or three nights that week and he never needed to use his pup tent after all.

CHAPTER TWENTY FOUR:
Mud baths

The next time I visited that part of northern California—Napa County—where I had ridden along with Greg Cowden in his little Citroen Deux-Chevaux convertible, was another beastly hot summer day. It might have been that same amazing summer of Greg or it might have been the next year. I can only try to write what I remember and time gets slippery at such a distance. Still, some memories are permanently etched in a shadowy attic of my brain like a stash of sticky old faded porn. Others have simply been lost to time or sparks of moments that still come up in the rare occasional wet dream.

It was a midweek day, I'm sure of that much. I was with a bunch of other resort workers who all had the day off too and one of them owned a pick-up truck with a camper on the back. He was the only one I didn't really know, a tall, dark, and very sexy guy. Someone else rode up front with him on the way to Calistoga. I rode in the back with five other bartenders and waiters, so there were eight of us. It seems to me that we had to have an even number of people when we made our reservations for the mud baths.

If the heat was bad outside, it was even worse in that camper with the sun beating down on its tin roof. I don't know why we didn't bring along a couple of six-packs of cold beer, at least. Maybe it was because it was only midmorning when we left. We could drink water from the tap in the camper's sink, but it was warm and tasted like the pipes it was sitting in. We did have one thing to drink on our way to Calistoga, though. Someone in our group had brought along a thermos, the biggest one they make, the kind that sits on a shelf or a picnic table and has a little plastic spigot on the side. The only trouble was that he had filled it with ice cold gin!

We drank it, of course. It tasted delicious once I got used to it. The six of us finished off all that gin and when we got to where we were going they could practically pour us out of the back door of that camper and onto the parking lot of the mud baths.

Even as drunk as I was, I noticed that the place was pretty tacky, maybe not pink flamingos and green plastic frogs tacky, but it hadn't been remodeled since the '60s and still desperately clung to those Eisenhower era colors and fabrics and tchotchkes.

The eight of us started out with showers and a soak in a hot tub that was big enough to hold us all. Then we were buried in mud, four at a time in individual coffins in the other end of the room. I remember that it felt wonderful as the attendants pushed me down and packed handfuls of mud on top of me. The mud is in fact volcanic ash mixed with mineral water and my body felt weightless in it. It also felt like every pore from head to toe opened up at the same time and all that gin oozed out. I'm surprised they let us in there, smelling the way we did. That mud must have been 40 proof after we got out of it.

The attendants scraped the mud off our bodies, back into the tanks. Then we took another shower and someone toweled me off and wrapped me in white sheets like a mummy and laid me down outside on a cot in the sun to sweat some more.

I don't remember what happened next. I just know that all eight of us had been naked together and there was no stress about that. I imagine we had all seen each other at some of the nude swimming pools at the gay resorts lots of times already.

Well, I shouldn't say there was *no* stress. I was excited to see the driver naked, the tall guy, the only one I didn't know at all before this trip. He didn't drink alcohol, but he liked pot, I discovered on the trip back when I rode up front in the cab of the truck with him. He liked pot a lot… and he told me he didn't mind getting a blow job while he was driving.

CHAPTER TWENTY FIVE:
Leather Weekend

I want to write about *Leather Weekend* at The Woods, but first I'm trying to remember how it came about and what all was involved. It wasn't built around any contest like the Drummer weekend or Mister Russian River, which both became annual events once I got them started. This was just a big crazy decadent weekend in the country for the South of Market crowd.

I remember that I borrowed a motorcycle to use as décor, suspended above the dance floor by chains. It took about eight of us to get it up there using graduated heights of scaffolding and ramps and then suspended from the giant Douglas Fir Poles that had framed the old Hexagon House ever since it was an art school called Pond Farm back in the 1940s. We even wired the headlight of the bike to the light board in the DJ booth so that it could turn on and off for special effects through fog, no doubt. Taking the motorcycle down after the event was over was a whole lot easier than getting it up there!

The only other décor was an old toilet bowl we had found behind one of the cabins. Al Knopka, another of the owners of The Woods, and I cleaned it up and put it on a tall pedestal, stuck a vase inside and three dozen long-stemmed red roses. It was lovely.

The back bar off the north side of the dance floor, which had once been a cocktail lounge with a roaring winter fireplace and a piano where Betty Hutton performed long ago, became a leather bar for the weekend. We plastered the walls with posters from famous leather bars from all over the country and showed hard-core gay porn, risking a citation from the State ABC (Alcohol Beverage Control) but it certainly set the mood for the weekend.

Someone, probably my buddy Gabriel, knew the owner of the mirror that had been over the bar at the Tool Box bar and he loaned it to us to put over our back bar for the weekend. The mirror was etched with a big muscular arm with a flexed bicep and a fist gripping a wrench. The Tool Box was one of the first leather bars in San Francisco, open from 1961-1971, so it was before my time, but it was notorious. *Life Magazine* ran a famous article called "Homosexuality in America" in their June 25, 1964 issue (no doubt for my birthday) showing the massive Chuck Arnett black and white mural depicting a group of tough-looking men. Several of the attendees of The Woods' Leather Weekend told me they were of an age to remember the bar and that the mirror brought back great memories for them.

The stunningly handsome Ray Perea, who was the first man to win the title of Mister Drummer—Val Martin was appointed by John Embry the first year and in later years the title was changed to International Mister Drummer—was living at the river with his partner Ski, so we got Ray to tend bar in his chaps and a harness to show off his buffed body to go with his truly charming and totally real personality. Everyone loved Ray!

Each of the leather bars in San Francisco rented a room or a cabin with lots of liquor and drugs so that when The Woods bars stopped serving alcohol at 2 a.m. (under California law) there was no end to the party. You just had to know someone and it didn't take long for everyone there to feel like they knew someone.

I borrowed a few slings and hung them up around the property. Two went in the pool house beside the Flintstone pool. Another one went in the two-car garage under one of the owners' cabins. Purveyors of sex toys, leather goods, and lubricants set up booths to sell their wares in the south side dining room for the weekend.

Billy Preston was the only musician who ever played with both The Beatles and The Rolling Stones. When he and his manager arrived at The Woods to perform at Leather Weekend it took them a while before they realized this was a gay resort. I don't know why they didn't know before he was booked, but by the time we finished his sound check, he laughed, expressed his surprise, and admitted that his "manager" was really his lover. Who knew that the man who sang "Nothing From Nothing" and "Will It Go Round In Circles" was gay? He sang and played keyboards and I really enjoyed his performance, but I didn't know until he died in 2006 that he had spent almost his entire career in the closet.

Saturday afternoon after Billy Preston's sound check I had some time to relax out by the south pool at The Woods where I met a friendly African-American woman and we got to talking. She told me her name was Mary and we had a nice visit, laughing about this, that, and everything in between, over sticky, slushy, strawberry daiquiris. She was so sweet I felt like we were instant old friends. I didn't take her for a lesbian but even if she were, it would have been unusual to see a single black female all by herself, so I finally asked her what she was doing alone at The Woods. She told me she was meeting up with an old friend of hers a little later, so I thought nothing more about it.

That night Billy Preston did a couple of high-energy songs and then announced that he wanted to bring someone up to the stage to do a number with him. "So please, everybody let's have a great big welcome for Merry Clayton!!" and the crowd at The Woods gave her a huge ovation.

Of course it was the same woman I had met earlier by the pool. I heard her say her name was "Mary" when we introduced ourselves, but that night I realized who she was. Merry Clayton was probably most famous for having sung the immortal "Gimme Shelter" duet with Mick Jagger on The Rolling Stones album.

Merry Clayton had debuted at 14 years old, recording "Who Can I Count On?" with Bobby Darin in 1962 and been one of Ray Charles' Raelettes. She sang background vocals for Neil Young, Tom Jones, Carole King, Joe Cocker, and others. In later years she would go on to act in television and films and provide some of the best songs in the movie *Dirty Dancing*. In 2013 she was featured in the Oscar winning documentary *Twenty Feet from Stardom*.

Billy Preston at the Leather Weekend at The Woods with friends Jerry Keller (c.), Mark Abramson (r.), who organized the event, and Mary Clayton of Rolling Stones fame. (Photo: Robert Pruzan)

Photo from the *Bay Area Reporter*

I followed Merry's career with great interest ever since that afternoon by the pool at The Woods and I've always been grateful that I got to spend that sweet time with her before I even knew who she was.

Billy Preston performed on Saturday night of Leather Weekend, but I wanted something new and different for Sunday T-Dance, some entertainment that the leather guys would really enjoy. A few weeks earlier, I had been down to the city visiting friends and someone invited me to the Nourse Auditorium to see an evening of men dancing. I don't know who produced this event or whether it ever happened again, but it was great! Many different kinds of dancing happened on that stage that night. There was no emcee, but all the acts were listed in the program. The only requirement, I guess, was that you had to be male and you had to do something you considered dancing. Some of them were solo acts, more of a gymnastic demonstration than a dance, I thought, but it was still fun to watch a nearly naked man with a far more developed body than most of us had. Gyms were still a rather new reality for most gay guys.

Four men in matching outfits did a snazzy tap-dance routine. Other dancers weren't very good at all, but the audience cheered for every act, no matter. Two of the acts I remember best because I went backstage and invited them to come up to the river and perform for my Leather Weekend at The Woods for the Sunday T-Dance entertainment.

One group was the Barbary Coast Cloggers. Clogging is a bit like tap dancing, but for big, really butch guys. It is North America's indigenous dance form, also called step dancing, growing out of the Appalachian Mountains. Ron Brewer was a bartender at the Pilsner Inn on Church Street and my contact person for the group.

When they came out onto the middle of the dance floor that Sunday afternoon, the leather T-Dance crowd gathered in a circle all around them to watch and listen to the thunderous sounds they made, not only with their feet but with hoots and hollers. Their energy was infectious.

The other act I brought up to the river was a pas de deux performed by Randall Krivonic in full leather with a long black bullwhip in one hand and Ed Stark in full drag as a leather ballerina, complete with toe shoes. Their act was a combination of classical ballet and an Apache Dance, very rough and terribly funny, as the two dancers threw each other around. Ed Stark would become one of my closest friends and my boss a few years later.

Back stage at The Nourse, I hadn't recognized Ed in drag as a guy I had once met at the 21st Street Baths, who took me home to spend the night at his house on Vicksburg Street in Noe Valley. On that Sunday when he arrived at The Woods, out of costume, he looked vaguely familiar and then he reminded me of that night. I lost track of Randall Krivonic after that weekend at The Woods, but it turned out that Ed owned a bar at 469 Castro Street called (in order):

> The Club Unique
> The Nothing Special
> The Special
> Headquarters
> The Night Shift

It was said that The Club Unique had been a straight biker bar for years and that Janis Joplin used to hang out there to drink shots of Southern Comfort and shoot pool whenever she came over the hill from where she lived in the Haight/Ashbury district to Eureka Valley, which would soon be better known as simply "The Castro."

The story goes that Ed Stark and his partner Jack South rode their motorcycles out from Kansas City to San Francisco at some time in the late '60s or early '70s, looking for a bar to buy. The Castro was just beginning to turn gay when they walked into this funky, smoky bar called The Club Unique, just steps from the Castro Theater. Ed looked around and said, "Club Unique, huh? There's nothing special about this place!" So they bought the bar and gave it its new name, The Nothing Special.

The motorcycle we suspended over the dance floor
for Leather Weekend

Ed and Randall's leather ballet was also a big hit with the leather crowd that Sunday afternoon at The Woods. There are wide gaps in my memory of that weekend, no doubt due to an excessive use of drugs and alcohol, but I do remember that I had saved the best for last. Monday evening for Locals' Night I had Edith Massey there to perform. She was best known for playing Divine's mother Edie, the Egg Lady in John Waters' cult hit film *Pink Flamingos*.

A lot of the leather crowd stayed over an extra night just to catch Edie's act. I adored Edie. She was warm and kind and not nearly as stupid as she appeared in John Waters' movies. The only songs she sang that I can remember were "Big Girls Don't Cry" and "Punks, Get Off the Grass!"

From my AIDS memoir *For My Brothers*:

After her Monday evening performance, I ended up spending the rest of the night in the room adjacent to hers in a threesome with Edie's "manager" and his boyfriend who was acting as her "tour photographer." I wish we'd taken some pictures of that!

In the morning, I took the two of them and Edie to breakfast at the little café that was perched over Fife Creek. I ordered an omelet and Edie had pancakes. She said, "You know, Mark…I don't even like eggs. That Egg Lady thing was just for the movies. That was John's (Waters) idea."

I will never forget that amazing voice of hers, a nasal high-pitched shriek. That morning at breakfast, she also told me, "You know, Mark… I could afford to get teeth now, but John said it might ruin my image."

CHAPTER TWENTY SIX:
Family matters

No matter how much fun I might be having, no matter how debauched I have managed to make my life, every once in a while there are times when my biological family intervenes to remind me of where I came from and the "good boy" I always tried to be. I guess that good boy is always there, deep inside most of us, no matter how hard we try to escape him.

During my three-plus years at the river, I only had one visit from any of my biological family. My sister Joan and her husband Steve and their two little boys, my nephews Brad and Brian, flew down in their four-seater Cessna from Oregon. I remember driving in my pick-up truck to the Santa Rosa airport north of town, which was little more than a landing strip in those days. It must have been an uneventful visit because none of us can remember any details about it, all these many years later.

On the other hand, my only family crisis came in a series of phone calls from my parents to the blue house on Orchard Avenue. My mother called first to tell me that my Aunt Margaret from Iona was in the Slayton hospital because she'd had a heart attack. Margaret was the middle one of the seven sisters, the one who stayed in the family home that their father had built. She taught grade school in Chandler and cared for my grandmother until she died at 88 years of age when I was still in high school.

Mom told me she had sat by Margaret's side in the hospital until visiting hours were over and Margaret told her, "Go on home. Get some rest. Don't worry about me. I'll be fine." But it was always my mother's way to worry, so much so that she had to call me in California to relay this bit of news. I loved my Aunt Margaret, but I didn't worry and I got a good night's sleep that night.

The next evening, my mother called me in tears to tell me that Aunt Margaret had had another heart attack during the night, a much bigger one, and that this one had killed her. Then Mom started sobbing so hard into the telephone that my father had to take it from her. He told me that he'd better hang up because she needed him at that moment far more than I did.

They called me every few days after that. I don't remember who was the executor of Aunt Margaret's estate, but my parents lived the closest to Iona of any of Mom's sisters, so they drove over there every day to sort through all of the things in that home where my mother spent her childhood, a lifetime of cherished antiques and memories.

This was the same house where my mother had descended the grand open staircase on her wedding day and married my father at the foot of the stairs in the dining room filled with friends and family. After the ceremony, they all went outside for a reception in my grandmother's beautiful flower gardens.

It seems almost peculiar now, looking back, how differently everyone grieves. As I said, I loved my Aunt Margaret, but I was 2,000 miles away and so concerned with my mother's emotions that I hardly took time to process my own.

Each phone call brought news of something else they had run across, a tin toy from my mother's childhood, a scarf, a brooch, and gallon jars full of buttons my grandmother had saved when she tore old clothing into long strips of fabric to wind onto wooden shuttles to make rag rugs on her loom in the cellar.

Most phone calls ended with my mother in tears, dad taking the phone from her and finishing up the conversation with me. It's odd that I don't remember ever hearing my mother cry after that, even when my dad died nearly twenty years later, but I wasn't there at the time. She probably did, or maybe her life was all cried out. She was always such a strong woman that her tears frightened me, but life went on.

CHAPTER TWENTY SEVEN:
Gorgeous George

One Sunday I arrived at The Woods a couple of hours early so that I could hang out with some friends at the clothing-optional pool before I had to start work bartending at T-Dance. It was always so quiet and peaceful beside the pools at The Woods in the mornings and early afternoons, especially on weekdays, but it could be pleasant on weekends too before the disc jockey started spinning records and cranked the music up for dancing.

It could be downright serene except for one thing. The Sony Walkman had come on the market in 1979, so it was still a fairly new concept in the early '80s. It fit into a shirt pocket and people could listen to their own choice of music on headphones wherever they went. They sold for around $150, which would be nearly $500 today, when adjusted for inflation. Most of the people who could afford to stay at The Woods could afford a Walkman and the price was probably already coming down by then too.

I never owned a Walkman, but I can remember many times when I was lying in the sun by the pool when someone across the way from me was listening to theirs and, unable to contain themselves, they burst out singing along to music only they could hear… at top volume and usually off key. It made everyone else around the pool laugh out loud every time it happened and reminded me why I never wanted a Walkman.

This particular Sunday I was enjoying my friends, taking a break from a cutthroat game of Parcheesi, when I stood up to stretch and smoke a cigarette.

Have I mentioned it enough times, how nearly everyone I knew smoked cigarettes (among other things) then? I quit smoking years ago and find it a fairly disgusting habit now, not to mention the cash drain on people who are hooked on nicotine and can't afford it, so it surprises me to look back on those times when I was so young and healthy and picture a cigarette between my fingers. I can still remember the satisfaction of my first cigarette of the day, sucking that smoke deep into my lungs, a jolt of sheer pleasure like the first line of coke off the mirror, up the straw through my nose and dripping down my throat. I haven't done cocaine in a long time either.

Anyway…I was standing there smoking a cigarette beside the tall wooden wall that surrounded the deck around the nude pool when I noticed a stunning young man doing a handstand on the patch of lawn between the pool and the back parking lot. He was barefoot and bare-chested with longish blond hair as soft as feathers framing his handsome face. He had on a pair of baggy gray shorts, so when he was upside down, gravity exposed that he was also wearing a very full jockstrap under them. Now he was walking on his hands across the grass, then doing back flips and cartwheels like an Olympic gymnast.

I was spellbound, but it was time for me to go to work so I took one more dip in the pool and headed across the little footbridge over Fife Creek to get the patio bar set up. I was certain that I would see that beautiful young man again.

We were a couple of hours into T-Dance when I spotted that gorgeous blond I'd seen earlier. He was still bare-chested on the dance floor with a pale blue tank top tucked into the belt loop of his tight blue jeans. He had on cowboy boots that made him about six feet tall and he was a terrific dancer. I kept on slinging drinks on automatic pilot, not wanting to take my eyes off of him.

He finally came out to the patio bar and ordered a beer from me, which I comped him, of course. I flirted with him shamelessly, told him I'd been watching his calisthenics on the lawn earlier and found him so very hot.

He told me his name was George and that he had, in fact, been a gymnast in high school and college. He wasn't one to brag, but when I asked, he admitted that he'd won lots of awards and an athletic scholarship, but now he was working for one of the largest brokerage firms in the country at their office in San Francisco's financial district. That sounded boring, but I invited him home anyway.

George said he was staying with a couple of friends in a cabin they'd rented at Fern Grove, across the road from Fife's. His friends were driving back to the city that night for work in the morning, but for some reason George had Monday off. I told him I'd be glad to drive him back to the city after he spent the night with me on Orchard Avenue.

George was an excellent kisser. His whole body was perfectly tanned and toned, nearly hairless without an ounce of extra body fat. He was excellent at a lot of things, but mostly I just wanted his incredible ass and he was fine with that. I loved fucking him, kissing him, holding him, and when I got up to go to the bathroom I could hardly wait to get back to bed.

I stopped, though. I stood in my bedroom doorway to look at him, lying there naked on my bed facing away from me, arms bent around his head, legs spread slightly apart. The moonlight coming in through the window spread dim light across his big round shoulders and made the muscles of his glutes seem to glow in the dark.

I didn't own a camera in those days, but I stood there long enough to take a mental picture because the beauty of his body took my breath away. I wasn't sure if I would ever again in my life see anything as perfect as this guy named George asleep in the moonlight on a hot summer night and I never wanted to forget it.

We slept late the next day. I made coffee and we drank it out by the pool at the blue house. Bobby and Jonathan and Bob had all driven back to the city on Sunday night, so it was just the two of us, George and me. He floated on an air mattress while I went back inside to make toast and bacon and eggs.

The day was already turning into a scorcher and we were in no hurry so I took Highway One, all the way down through Bodega Bay past Point Reyes, through Stinson Beach and past Mt. Tamalpais. It was even hot at the coast, so we drove with our shirts off, windows wide open. We pulled over at one of the scenic overlooks to get out of the truck and stretch. We were high above the Pacific Ocean and no one else was around. I pointed to a path that led down a steep trail with bushes on both sides and George smiled, leading the way downhill a few yards and out of sight of anyone who might park up above. He stopped and stood there, staring out at the ocean. I pulled down his shorts and got inside him with nothing but spit for lube. I wrapped my arms around his chest with my fingers tweaking his nipples and we both came at the same time. His load shot into the air and all over the bushes below us and mine burst deep inside of him.

George came up to the river almost every weekend for the rest of that summer. He stayed with me on Orchard Avenue and got to know Jon and Bobby and Bob, even though George was a little shy around new people. I don't think my friends liked him very much. Maybe they were jealous of his good looks or jealous of me because I got to sleep with him or maybe they resented the time he took me away from them.

I didn't care. It didn't really matter. When the season was over, so was my fling with George. It was fine. We were never in love with each other. It was just great sex. He was a stockbroker, for crying out loud!

I never saw him when I came down to San Francisco and went to the bars and dance clubs. I don't know where he hung out or if he went out at all in the city. I never saw George at the river the following season or ever again. Maybe he met someone and fell in love. All I know is that he was still in San Francisco for a while after we stopped seeing each other. When the *B.A.R.* started publishing obituaries every week because so many of us were dying of AIDS, George was one of the first people I recognized.

The clothing-optional pool

CHAPTER TWENTY EIGHT:
Christine Jorgensen

The entertainers who performed at The Woods on Monday nights "Locals' Night" in the cabaret setting were the ones I usually got to know better than the Saturday night disco stars who came to Guerneville. Since I was the maitre'd for their shows, I not only seated the audience, but also acted as a liaison between the backstage dressing room and the sound and light operators in the DJ booth. I would fetch drinks from the bar if they liked or anything else they needed. Kleenex? Paper towels? An ashtray? A coke straw?

One of the many Monday night performers I got to meet was, by then world-famous, Christine Jorgensen, the first person to become widely known in the United States for having sex reassignment surgery in her 20s.

Having grown up on a farm, transsexuals were not something we learned about in school or discussed over the dinner table. Neither was the existence of gay people in the world. So I don't know how I had always known who Christine Jorgensen was, ever since I was a child. I must have seen her on the news or in the newspapers. She'd had the surgery in Denmark, leaving George

Jorgensen behind and starting a whole new life as Christine before I was even born.

She arrived at The Woods on Monday afternoon for sound check and I introduced myself, assuring her that I would be there for her before, during, and after her show. She didn't need much help backstage, but we set up a large folding screen on the stage. It was just tall enough so that her head stuck out, so she could do all her costume changes while she continued to talk to the audience.

Christine's show was pretty corny, as I remember it, with a Tallulah Bankhead impression and a little Hollywood gossip. At one point she came out from behind the screen dressed as Superwoman with a big red "S" across her chest and a cape hanging from her shoulders while she sang Helen Reddy's 1971 hit "I am woman, hear me roar!"

She didn't have a great singing voice, but she did a few other songs in her act, including "I Enjoy Being a Girl," of course. I warned you it was corny. I can't remember now whether she traveled with a pianist or sang to a taped background track. Her stories were the better part of her act and she did a bit of a Q&A session with the audience. She had a great sense of humor and seemed very comfortable laughing at herself, perhaps learning from all her years in public life that people had been laughing at her, in many cases. If she was to be the butt of any joke, she would be the one to tell it. She put everyone at ease in that way and I respected her for it.

I've known lots of transwomen and a few transmen since then. Living in San Francisco all these years, and especially in the Castro, they are our neighbors and our friends, but I have to admit that meeting my first transperson, Christine Jorgensen was a bit of a curiosity to me.

After the show, she and I sat down at one of the bars with my friend Bob. He always drove a Jeep, but I remember distinctly that the two of them got into a lengthy conversation about Cadillacs, the only kind of car Christine would ever drive. When people came up to ask for pictures with her, she couldn't have been more gracious. When they asked for an autograph, she signed one of her old 5x7 glossies from a stack of headshots that she pulled from her large, black, hard-sided purse. In that picture she was decades younger. I wouldn't have recognized the girl in the black and white profile as the same person as this elegant older blonde lady dripping with jewelry, sitting on a bar stool beside me.

Christine liked me, for some reason. She was charming and a lovely person to talk with; she seemed as familiar to me as one of my elderly Minnesota aunts. She told me she was stopping in San Francisco for a couple of days before she went back down south to her place in Laguna Beach. I think she was staying at the Fairmont Hotel on Nob Hill. I mentioned that I was going to be down in the city that week too and she asked for the phone number where I was staying with my friend Roger on Seward Street above the Castro.

Sure enough, she called me there the following Tuesday morning after Roger had left for work. She told me that she was hosting a few of her oldest and dearest friends in San Francisco for lunch at the Cliff House and invited me to join them. As things turned out, I didn't join them and I never saw Christine Jorgensen again. I think I had a dental appointment or maybe I just made one up as an excuse.

It was one thing to be nice to people at work, I might have thought, but when I went down to the city it was to see friends and go to the gay bars and have all the debauchery I wanted at the baths. Or maybe I was feeling too shy, afraid that I would be intimidated by her "oldest and dearest" ones who were probably all her age while I was still in my twenties. What could I possibly have to say that would be of interest to any of them?

All these years later, I could kick myself for not going. It might have been fascinating to just be quiet and listen to them talk. I might have learned something and it would have been a wonderful story to add to this book. I don't remember anything about getting laid that week, but I'm sure I would have remembered that lunch at The Cliff House. Now I'll never know. Christine Jorgensen, a heavy smoker, died of lung cancer on May 3, 1989, in a hospital in San Clemente, California, just a few years after I met her.

Christine Jorgensen

CHAPTER TWENTY NINE:
Charles Pierce

O f all the wonderful performers I got to know when I worked at The Woods Resort, Charles Pierce was one of my favorites. I always thought of him as a brilliant comic first and a drag queen second. I think he preferred the term "male actress," but whatever you called him, he was a very kind and clever man.

B.A.R. ad from the early '70s

Toward the end of his career he was packing them in at the Venetian Room at the Fairmont, Davies Hall, and the Opera House. The first time I saw him perform was at the old City/Cabaret on Montgomery and Broadway in about 1975. Upstairs was a big gay disco and downstairs was the show room.

Charles was still working with his sidekick Rio Dante at that time. I remember the first part of the show they had their heads sticking out from little doll-puppet bodies that they moved with their hands to make them dance while they sang and joked around. That was a leftover from the days when there were still laws against cross dressing.

The finale was Charles as Jeanette MacDonald in a swing covered with flowers and lights that twinkled as he sang "San Francisco" and swung out over the audience. I wasn't there that particular night, but legend has it that he once caught the toupee of a man in the front row on one of his high heels. Charles didn't miss a beat. He pulled the rug off his shoe and the next time he swung forward he plopped it back onto the bald guy's head.

Before I met Charles at the Russian River, I also saw him at The Plush Room of the York Hotel. My friend Roger knew him and insisted on sticking around to say hello after the show. We were four in our group, the only people left in the place who weren't employees, by the time Charles came out in a suit and tie and Roger introduced us all.

When Charles first arrived at The Woods, one of the owners introduced him to me and explained that I would be the maître'd for his shows there. Charles said, "I know Mark. I met you at the Plush Room with Roger Pascoe and your friends Bob and Gerald." He had a mind like that! He remembered everything and everybody.

This was the early '80s. The Reagans were in the White House. Actually, they had been hosting Queen Elizabeth and Prince Philip in San Francisco earlier that year. One afternoon during Charles' run, I saw a car pull up to the front of the resort and Charles popped out. He said, "Mark, look what I found!" He handed me a matronly-looking dress on a hanger. "Help me carry this stuff inside, would you?" He ducked into the back seat of the car and pulled out several shopping bags.

"Where have you been?"

"Thrift store shopping, except for these," he showed me a bag with reflective plastic numerals in it, the kind you might put on your front door to show your address. "I bought these at the Guerneville Five and Dime."

Inside his dressing room, he showed me the rest of his "finds"—a dowdy wig, a rhinestone tiara, a pair of sensible shoes and a big square plastic purse. That night the queen of England appeared in his show for the first time. The purse was decorated with those reflective stickers spelling out "QE II" on one side and "HRH" on the other. One of his jokes was: "Diana is expecting and they've already chosen a name for the baby. They're calling it 'Up.' Can you imagine? 'Here they come... Up, Chuck, and Di!"

Even when his jokes were corny and bad, Charles was so loveable that we all laughed anyway.

My old roommate Emilio, whom I had left behind in our apartment on 19TH and Douglas when I moved to the Russian River, was several years older than me. He had told me about when he and a group of his friends used to drive down to the nude beach at San Gregorio on Saturday afternoons in the '60s. The northern end of the beach is covered with driftwood that people have arranged to form little shelters. We used to call them condos. Emilio said that he and his pals usually ended up in one that was right next door to Charles Pierce and his group. They were all very friendly, sharing corkscrews, passing joints back and forth, rubbing suntan lotion into each other's backs.

Emilio saw Charles perform too, of course, back in the days of The Black Cat and The Purple Onion. When I told Emilio that Charles was coming to The Woods, he decided to drive up to the Russian River for a couple of days and catch his act. He had a friend with him that night, I think it was the last night of Labor Day weekend, and I seated Emilio and his friend at a little cocktail table one row back from and dead center stage.

Just before the show started, the lights were already dimming, I was standing at the back of the showroom when Val Diamond came running in through the side door. "Mark, I just drove up from the city and I've got to see Charles. Can you fit me in somewhere?"

"Of course!" I grabbed a bentwood chair from the dining room and held it over my head as I led Val through the sold-out room and told Emilio and his friend to "scootch over" a little bit so that she could join them at their table.

One of my tasks as maître'd, especially for Charles' shows, was to let him know if there was anyone famous in the audience. I remember him introducing the pianist Peter Mintun one night. He was so adorable with his wavy hair and cute shy smile! Another night Peter Pender came to the show. He owned Fife's, our biggest competitor, and he was a World Champion bridge player.

Charles started the show in a blonde wig and his first bit was mostly one-liners from a string of famous blondes from Marilyn Monroe:

"My boyfriend has terrible dandruff. Someone told me to give him Head and Shoulders. How do you give shoulders?"

…to Carol Channing:

"I went to the zoo the other day with Doris Day's sister Doo-Dah (pause)…*Yes*, Doo-Dah Day! I told the zookeeper I'd like to see the monkeys. Could you tell them Carol's here? He said they were in the back of their cages, mating. I said, do you suppose they'd come out if I offered them a banana? He said, Would *you*? I said, Yeeessh!"

… to Barbara Stanwyck, but he mostly talked about her, rather than doing an impression of her. "Where, in Stockton, California, do you buy a leather pantsuit in 1830?" And "Poor Barbara Stanwyck. She lost the ranch anyway… she couldn't keep her calves together!"

It was a more innocent time, I guess, and Charles could be edgy and "naughty" without much concern for political correctness. He joked about seeing Pia Zadora starring in a play as Anne Frank. Her acting was so terrible that when the Nazis showed up, everyone in the audience yelled, "She's in the attic!"

As Katherine Hepburn, "Poor Patti Page… that doggie in the window was just her reflection!… Well, I wanted to do a scene for you from my latest film, 'On Goldie Hawn.' No…that wasn't it, was it? 'On Golden Pond!' Jane, come and do your famous back flip off the diving board before we all go suckface…" And if "suckface" didn't get a big laugh right away, Charles chastised the audience, "You didn't see the picture, did you!?"

When Charles went backstage to change into Mae West, I ran to tell him that Val Diamond was in the second row center. I knew he would want to make a fuss over her. At some point in the Mae West segment, still in character, he announced, "Ladies and Gentlemen, we have a very special guest in the audience tonight, the star of *Beach Blanket Babylon*, Val Diamond! Stand up and take a bow, Val!"

The house lights came up and everyone applauded, but before the lights went back down, Charles continued pointing at Val's table and shouted at Emilio, "And *you*! I haven't seen you in twenty years and this is the first time you've ever had a stitch of clothes on!"

⌐

Each of Charles' four shows at The Woods that weekend was the same—that is to say that the same leading ladies appeared in the same order—but there were always surprises, such as the Queen Elizabeth bit. Charles was also so brilliant at ad-libs and working the live audience that we never knew what might happen. I think that was a lot of his appeal over the years. You could go back to see him again and again, even hear him tell some of the same jokes over and over, and still laugh just as hard as you did the first time you heard them. It was a joy just to be in his presence. When he was on stage he was obviously having as much fun "working" as we were having just being in his audience.

Charles ended each of those shows with Bette Davis, which was probably his best known portrayal of them all. Google him sometime: "Charles Pierce as Mae West" and laugh out loud. At one point in the show, Bette Davis announced, "Now I need a cocktail! Would someone be a darling and fetch me a cocktail, please!?"

Gabriel Starr was working the bar off to the north side of the main room, closest to the stage, so he always had the cocktail ready to send up to the lip of the stage with one of the cocktail waiters, an oversize stemmed martini glass filled with chilled vodka and several twists of lemon peel. Charles took the glass, thanked the waiter, and then he started plucking the lemon twists out with his fingertips and tossing them out toward the audience cursing, "What are Cher's fingernail clippings doing in my drink!?"

One afternoon, Gabriel and Charles and I were sitting out on The Woods' patio next to Fife Creek, having cocktails, telling stories, and having silly fun. Charles did most of the talking, but Gabe and I had stories too, and plenty of questions to prod him to continue his wonderful tales. This weekend was his first time playing The Woods, so I asked him how he felt about being there. I knew that some performers liked to do their act and flee right back to the city or the airport, while others liked to relax and enjoy their time in the great outdoors. Charles didn't have the option of going very far, since he was with us for four days.

He told us he'd spent the previous afternoon visiting some old friends who were encamped at the Bohemian Grove. Neither Gabe nor I had ever been inside, so that was interesting. He gave me his friends' names, so I made sure they got ringside seats that night.

Charles told us that he stayed up late after his shows, sitting alone in his hotel room—the infamous room #20—reading with the bedside lamp turned on. He sounded quite lonely for a moment, but then he smiled and got a twinkle in his eye and told Gabriel and me that he had a confession to make. Each night he had been at The Woods he'd had a charming late-night visitor, a very sexy young man named John.

Gabriel and I both had the same thought at the same time. "John, the gardener?"

"Why, *yes!*" Charles replied in Carol Channing's voice. "John, the lovely gardener!"

John was a simple, unassuming young man, a real "country boy," who rarely spoke unless he was spoken to. I hardly ever heard him say more than two words except when he'd show up asking for a beer from me when he was getting off work in the afternoon and that was such a rare occurrence that I didn't even charge him the employee price. "That's on the house, John…"

"Thank ya," he'd say with a nod of his head and wander off again.

I rarely saw John because he started work so early in the morning. He must have showed up around 4 a.m. to turn on the water sprinklers on the lawn around the front pool next to the hotel building. That would give the grass enough time to dry before people came out to sunbathe in the afternoon. Charles had

seen John outside his open patio door and invited him inside…
night after night.

John never came to the shows at night, so he would have had
no idea who Charles Pierce was. I'm not sure which one of the
three of us—probably Gabe—suddenly had a great idea. He found
John working on the grounds somewhere and asked him if he'd
like to make an easy twenty bucks that night. All he had to do was
show up at the back bar and bring one drink up to the performer
at a precise time during "her" show. I don't know where, but we
found him a tuxedo that fit him, too.

That night, John showed up on time and got dressed and
carried the drink on the silver tray, but Charles didn't take the
drink right away. Instead, he insisted that John come around to the
two or three stair steps and climb up to join him on stage.

I wish I could remember what Charles said to him—all in the
voice of Bette Davis, of course—but it was hilarious. He had John
turn around so that Charles could lift the tails of his jacket and
show off his big beefy buns in those tight tuxedo pants and the
audience loved it!

I had a newfound respect for John the gardener after that
night. He was so stoical that he didn't react at all to Charles'
shenanigans. He never let on that he had been having sex with
this Bette Davis interpreter for the past three nights. Maybe he just
thought, "Twenty bucks is twenty bucks." He might not even have
known who Bette Davis was, much less Charles Pierce. Maybe he
never did figure it out and it was the first time I ever noticed that
he really did have a great ass.

In later years I heard stories of Charles holding court with
Bea Arthur for long afternoons at the Patio Café on Castro Street
whenever the two of them were in town. Long after Charles was
retired from performing, he did an interview for the local San
Francisco gay newspaper, the *B.A.R.* in which one of the topics

was the last time he did drag. He said it was a Halloween party at Phyllis Diller's house and that he and Bea Arthur went together, both of them dressed in turbans as Norma Desmond from *Sunset Boulevard*.

Later still, I saw Bea Arthur in her touring one-woman show at the Alcazar Theatre in San Francisco and she told a funny story about a mother's visit to her gay son and his "roommate" and a missing silver soup ladle. She said that she had told the story at her dear friend Charles Pierce's funeral. Charles died on May 31, 1999.

Charles Pierce greeting card as Bette Davis

CHAPTER THIRTY:

The Frenchman and the movie star mystery

One Sunday T-Dance I served a drink to a very cute guy I'd never seen before. Besides being cute, he had a thick French accent and I've always been a sucker for accents, especially European ones.

He was about 5' 9", a little shorter than me, with jet black hair and a mischievous grin. We made eye contact for so long that it became almost embarrassing, so I asked him his name.

"Patrick," he said, but his accent made it sound almost as if the stress was on the second syllable. "Pat-reek." I shook his hand.

"I am Mark. Where are you from?" I asked.

"Marseilles… in France… but I live in San Francisco now. I am a chef."

"Nice to meet you!"

"You too, Marc." He didn't spell out my name, of course, but I just knew he would spell it with a "C" instead of a "K," which he always did when he left me a note during that summer we dated. He was wild in bed! I had just met my match in terms of horniness, stamina, and enthusiasm.

Patrick showed up at nearly every Sunday T-Dance from then on. He had to work Saturday nights in the city, so he drove up on

Sunday mornings and spent Sunday nights in my bed on Orchard Avenue. Sometimes he stayed through Monday nights too. It was fun showing him around the area, which he said reminded him of some parts of France. On Monday nights I would sneak him into cabaret shows at the last minute and we would share a tiny table in the back of the room once I got everyone seated. If the show was sold out, we could pull in a couple of stools from the bar or just stand and watch.

Patrick lived with a roommate on States Street, the longest street in San Francisco with no stop signs, or so I've been told by several cab drivers over the years. It's a quick short-cut over the hill between the Castro and the Haight.

I remember one dinner party he invited me to on States Street. Patrick was doing all the cooking and the dinner table was beautifully set for six people. As the guests arrived, one at a time, they all turned out to be gay men about the same age as Patrick and me, late twenties, early thirties, and all of them French. And cute!

Everyone was friendly enough and politely translated whatever they said to Patrick and to each other into English for me. Then cocktails were consumed, plus delicious courses of wonderful food and everyone was talking so fast that the English translations were soon forgotten. At first I was mildly annoyed, but they were a group of drunken gay Frenchmen, after all, laughing and eating and gesturing over the candlelit dinner and stemmed crystal wine glasses. I grew not to care as much that I couldn't understand their words. It was fun just to be there at that table absorbing their energy and their sexy "otherness" from the guys I was used to socializing with.

One Sunday after T-Dance at The Woods, Patrick mentioned something about a problem with his being able to stay and work in the United States. He actually used the words "get married," but I didn't think too much about it at the time. I was in a hurry for the two of us to get naked!

Every weekend from then on, he told me more and more about his plans and I gradually began to understand that he was serious. He was going to marry a woman so that he could stay in the country and get his citizenship. She was some friend of a friend. He hadn't even met her yet, but her name was Karen and she lived in L.A. She was coming up to San Francisco soon to work out the details for their union at City Hall. Then he would no longer have to worry about work visas and the government breathing down his back.

I didn't figure that all this marriage talk would make much of a difference in my relationship with Patrick. We were only together for one or two nights a week, anyway. Then one week he said, "I can't come up to see you next weekend, Marc."

"Why not?"

"Karen, my fiancée, she comes to the city to sign some papers and we picks out our wedding rings."

I loved hearing his accent so much that I scarcely listened to his words. Life went on. I'm sure I was still bringing other guys to my bed on Orchard Avenue in the meanwhile. Patrick came up on the weekend after ring shopping and told me that his new "bride" was lots of fun. She had picked out the dress that she would wear and they had a great time shopping and laughing together.

But… on Sunday afternoon he wanted to take her to the I-Beam on Haight Street for their T-Dance. That made sense to me, since he couldn't come to the river. When I had lived in the city, before I moved to the river, I rarely missed Sunday T-Dance at the I-Beam. The I-Beam was still in its hey-day when I knew Patrick.

Then he said, "But ve have to leave zee I-Beam almost right away. Too many people, zay bozzer her."

"What do you mean, bother her? She doesn't like crowds?"

"No, not zat. Karen and I, we just wanted to dance, but all these other people, they recognize her and they want to bozzer her for autographs."

"Recognize her from where? What are you talking about?"

"I think she is well-known in your country."

"For what?"

"She make film, but only in English, so I never see them."

"Films? You mean movies?"

"Yes, she is film actress in your country."

"What films? Which movies has she made?"

"She tells me some names, but I don't know zem. One was with Bette Davis. Something like burned offering? Something like that... and come back to fives and tens? What does this mean?"

"Come Back to the Five and Dime, Jimmy Dean?"

"Yes, that's it!"

"You're marrying Karen Black?"

"Yes, Karen Black. I thought I told you."

"You said her name was Karen. You never told me Karen Black!"

Even as I write these words, I know that people will think I made up this whole story or that I have switched from writing memoir to writing fiction. I know that you can look online at every entry on IMDB, Wikipedia, movie star magazines and biographies and never find any mention of Karen Black ever being married to a cute gay chef from Marseilles, France after her third divorce. I know because I've tried. She was (I can only assume happily) married when she died in 2013, so there is no way to ask her. I can only tell this story the way I remember it.

One morning I woke up in Patrick's bed on States Street after spending a rare night with him in the city. He was in the shower when the phone rang so he yelled out at me to pick it up. A woman was on the line. I told her, "Patrick is in the shower. Can I take a message?

"Thanks," she said. "Just tell him Karen called. He can call me back whenever… nothing urgent. He has my number."

"Okay, I'll tell him."

"Thanks again… bye."

I hung up the phone, of course, but what I really wanted to do was scream into it, "Wait! Don't hang up! Are you really Karen Black? I'm a huge fan of yours!"

Instead, I forced myself to act as naturally as I knew how. When Patrick asked who it was on the phone, I said, "It was just Karen. No biggie. Call her back when you get a chance."

I didn't see Patrick for a long time after his wedding at City Hall. I certainly hadn't been invited or I could have met this person in the flesh who was claiming to be Karen Black the film actress. Patrick was a changed man after that. He never came up to the river on Sundays anymore, but the season had wound down anyway. When I called him on the phone, he said he was sorry, but he also sounded scared. He told me that he was paranoid about the government finding out his marriage to Karen wasn't a "real" one.

Karen had gone back to Los Angeles, but from time to time she had to come up to San Francisco so that the two of them could appear together as a couple during the process of his acquiring citizenship. I didn't question him. I wasn't in his shoes, but still, it was a bit like watching someone stepping backward into the closet.

I didn't see Patrick for months after that, maybe even a year or two. I guess he got his citizenship eventually and got a divorce from Karen. According to Wikipedia, her last "official" marriage to Stephen Eckelberry was about four years later on September 27, 1987.

I ran into Patrick one day at the Pilsner Inn on Church Street, shortly after I had moved back to the city. He told me he was working in a restaurant and he could use some part-time help in the kitchen. I was only working part-time bartending jobs, so I took him up on it. The place was called the Fireside Café at 525 Castro Street, right next door to the Sausage Factory, where the Levi's store is today.

My favorite memory of that place had to do with Judy Garland, as gay as that sounds. For background music the restaurant used big old reel-to-reel tapes that seemed to play for hours without having to change the reels. Somewhere in the middle of one of them was Judy singing "The Man That Got Away" from the 1954 movie version of *A Star is Born*. The rule in the restaurant was that whenever that song came on, all the waiters and busboys and whoever was out on the floor had to stop what they were doing and grab something—a soup ladle, a wire whisk, a butter knife, anything to use as a pretend microphone—and lip-sing along for a bit. It was hysterical, especially when they got to the lines, "Good riddance, goodbye! Every trick of his you're on to! But fools will be fools, and where's he gone to?"

It was fun working side-by-side with Patrick in the kitchen. We laughed a lot. He was "married" to a man by this time, an Englishman whose name I can't remember. Unlike Patrick, his new lover had no sense of humor. I never understood what they saw in each other. Maybe it was just my presence, but whenever the three of us were in the same room together, I didn't feel that either of them was very happy. And sometimes when the Brit was out of town, Patrick and I would get together for sex again, just for old time's sake. Patrick was always fun in bed!

Tab Hunter and Divine in publicity still for *Lust in the Dust*

CHAPTER THIRTY ONE:

Divine

I didn't really get to know Divine until 1983 when he came to the Russian River to perform at The Woods. He appeared on Saturday night on the stage above the packed dance floor as the disco diva Divine to sing a couple of his hits, "Jungle Jezebel" and "Born to be Cheap." Then on Monday night he did his cabaret act for Locals' Night which was also standing room only.

I had seen Divine in the John Waters movies, of course, and a few times in person, first in Chicago when John Preston and I took the train down from St. Paul for a holiday weekend. On our way to the leather bars, John wanted to stop at a gay club (I think it was called The Baton) for a drink and probably to get in out of the cold. There was a huge drag queen swinging her enormous body around the stage and belting out a song with a voice that sounded like she'd gargled with gravel. John said it was Divine, but we were so far from the stage I wouldn't swear to it.

I was also with John Preston a few years later on a trip to New York when we saw Divine in an Off-Broadway play called *Neon Woman*. This was after both of us had moved from Minneapolis to San Francisco and John was becoming famous as a writer. I barely remember the play, but I'm sure we had some laughs before we headed on to the high point of that evening. John had scored us two free passes to a New Year's Eve party at Man's Country Baths. All the Colt Studios models from the coming year's calendar were there at the party in their muscled fleshy fineness. Once that party got going, I might have said, "Divine who?"

On Sunday afternoon of the "Divine" weekend at The Woods, about 1 p.m., I was lying out by the Flintstones' pool. I didn't have to start bartending until T-Dance started at 4, so I was working on my tan line. There were two or three dozen people in and around that pool on a hot lazy summer afternoon among the redwoods and at some point I looked up and noticed that everyone was gathering outside room #20. More and more people were leaving their towels behind to mark their territory, so I got up to join them. There was such a crowd I couldn't see over their heads, so I crouched down and got below them with my face almost pressed up against the glass.

Divine was on the bed, facedown, stark naked, getting fucked by some guy I'd never seen before. I'm sure all of us were silently thinking the same thing: "*Where* did she find *him*?" They were really going at it when I noticed a big round chocolate layer cake covered in creamy dark frosting on the bedside table. Divine reached over and dipped his left hand into the cake again and again and shoveled handfuls of it into his mouth like he was in hog heaven! We were all trying to stifle our giggles when Divine finally glanced over and saw us glued to the sliding glass doors. He seemed to be thrilled to be performing for this crowd of fans! He licked the frosting off the fingers of his left hand and used it to wave at us with a huge grin of chocolate-coated teeth. We all cheered and clapped and I think both of them must have climaxed at the same time. That was a sight I will never forget!

❦

Before I moved up to the Russian River, my last serious boyfriend in San Francisco was Kap Pischel and I knew that Divine was one of Kap's best friends. I remember a framed photograph on the desk in Kap's apartment on Frederick and Ashbury of Divine on water skis without make-up wearing a mumu. Kap told me he had taken the picture one summer while he was driving his family's speedboat on Fallen Leaf Lake near Tahoe. During the months when I was dating Kap, I kept missing out on meeting Divine whenever he was in town, but he always took time to see Kap. Maybe Divine was a little bit in love with Kap too. He was a gorgeous man.

The painful ending of my relationship with Kap was one of the reasons I moved up to the Russian River, whether I admitted it to myself at the time or not. I needed a fresh start.

It was Monday afternoon after we did a sound check for that night's performance when I really got to sit down and visit with Divi. That was what Kap always called him. I didn't bring up the fact that I had witnessed his performance the previous afternoon from outside the sliding glass doors of room #20. I did bring up Kap's name at some point and explained that I was the same Mark that Kap might have mentioned while I was "no doubt just one of a long stream of Kap's boyfriends" over the years.

"A cast of thousands!" Divine said with a laugh and then softened. "No, I do remember him talking about a guy named Mark. Something about a birthday party?"

"Yeah, that was the day he walked out of my life, my twenty-eighth birthday."

"I'm sorry," Divi said and I changed the subject. I told him I had gotten to know Edith Massey earlier that year when she performed at The Woods.

"Oh, *Dear* Edie!" Divine said with a grimace.

"I'm sorry. I shouldn't have brought her name up. Maybe you hate her. She never said anything bad about you, but we hardly talked about you at all."

"No, I don't hate her. No one can hate Edie. She tries so hard. It's just that it's so frustrating when we're on the set and we have to do take after take because Edie fucked up her lines and then she gets upset and starts to cry and John has to deal with her."

"I can only imagine," I said.

I had met Divine's manager Bernard Jay years earlier in San Francisco because he was a friend of a friend, but it was fun to get to know him a bit that weekend too. Years later he would write a wonderful book: *Not Simply Divine—beneath the makeup, above the heels, and behind the scenes with a cult superstar.* Bernard presented me with a Divine t-shirt that afternoon, so I quickly peeled off whatever I was wearing and tried it on. Divi grabbed a felt-tipped pen and was kind enough to autograph the shirt, front and back, while I was wearing it. We had a lot of laughs and I wore my new shirt that night when I was maître'd for the show. I still have the t-shirt but it hasn't fit me in years.

Divine's performance that night was amazing. He was a terrific comedian with brilliant timing. He eventually got around to singing "Native Love" and "You Think You're a Man" and "Shake it Up" and "The Name Game" and all the disco hits on his first album, but between the songs he told jokes and wonderful stories and bantered with the audience. He complained about how quiet it was out there in the country and said that the silence made it hard for him to fall asleep. He said, "I always sleep like a baby when there's a steady flow of sirens and buses and taxicabs below my windows, all of them honking their horns."

After the show, Divine dashed back to room #20 to take off his sparkly skin-tight dress and high heels and padding and came back to the bar in a caftan to hold court and sign autographs and pose for pictures with his fans for at least an hour. That was his last night at The Woods.

A half hour after he'd gone back to his room I remembered I was supposed to tell him about the plans for Tuesday morning, so I went over and knocked on the door of room #20. "Come in, come in, are you hungry?" Divine's hotel room dresser had been turned into a buffet complete with pork chops in gravy on a hotplate, mashed potatoes and Cole slaw and big bakery buns and butter. I saw no sign of chocolate cake. He must have finished that on Sunday after sex.

"Where did you get all this food?" I couldn't believe what I was seeing. Guerneville didn't even have a 24-hour Safeway yet in those days.

"Oh, I always plan ahead." Either Divine or Bernard must have made arrangements with one of the local restaurants earlier.

"Where is Bernard, anyway?"

"I don't know. He's either still at the bar or he's already gone to bed."

While we were eating, Divine told me about working on his most recent film *Lust in the Dust* with Tab Hunter, Lainie Kazan, and Cesar Romero. He said it was the most fun he'd ever had working on a movie because they were all out there in the desert together and everyone was gay—hair and make-up artists, cameramen, and all the cast and crew.

"Lainie Kazan is gay?" I asked. "My sister used to date some guy in Minneapolis who had just broken up with her. Maybe that was why--"

"No, not *her*! I don't mean the women, just the men!"

"Oh...sorry...anyway, I almost forgot the reason I came over here was to tell you that your car and driver will be here tomorrow morning at 10:30 to take you to the San Francisco airport. Thanks so much for dinner. The pork chops were delicious... and I'll see you in the morning. Goodnight!" I gave him a kiss on the cheek and left.

The next morning I made sure to get over to The Woods in time to say goodbye to Divine and Bernard. Divi looked almost like a little boy dressed in pastel shorts and short-sleeved shirt and enormous yellow-tinted sunglasses. Well, he looked like a very *big* little boy, but still sort of childlike, especially when compared to his wild stage and screen persona.

I never saw Divine again except in movies and once again on stage at the Alcazar Theater in San Francisco in *Women Behind Bars*. I don't know why I didn't go backstage that night and say hello. I followed his career, though. And I read somewhere that Divine was a big fan of Grave Line Tours in Hollywood, which took tourists in an old hearse to see the sites of famous celebrities' deaths.

Divine's last movie, *Hairspray* opened on February 15, 1988. Three weeks later, on March 7, 1988, he spent the day rehearsing to play Peg Bundy's Uncle Otto in an episode of the sitcom *Married With Children* which was to be taped the following day. That night he had dinner with friends at his hotel, the Regency Plaza Suites, and went to bed, where his heart stopped beating. He was buried, Harris Glenn Milstead, in Prospect Hill Cemetery, Towson, Maryland.

Years later, I was having drinks one afternoon at The Edge with Armistead Maupin. It was always fun to catch up with him and all the latest gossip when he and his husband Christopher Turner were my neighbors in the Castro. Armistead told me he'd heard they were making a movie out of *Hairspray,* the musical, and had finally cast someone to play Edna Turnblad, "one of the biggest closet cases in Hollywood," according to Armistead. I could only think how thrilled Divi would be to know that John Travolta was going to play the role that he'd created nearly twenty years earlier.

I also read that the owner of Grave Line Tours was grateful that Divine, one of his regular customers, died in a hotel that was already on his route. I'm sure that Divine would be glad to know that he'd been included in the tour.

My only other "Divine" story really has little to do with Divine, but it's a pretty good one. My old friend Don Nelson told me that when he was living in New York City in the early '70s he was dating an aspiring singer/dancer/actor/model who earned a living as a housekeeper while he waited for his big break. One of the people whose apartment he cleaned every week was Bette Midler and they got to be friends. One evening Nelson and his boyfriend took Bette to see this new movie everyone was talking about called *Pink Flamingos*. Afterward, walking Bette back to her apartment, Bette told them, "That dog shit scene was so disgusting! I might have to rethink this whole 'Divine Miss M' thing. I wouldn't want anyone to get us confused."

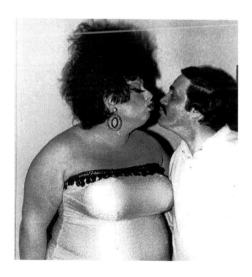

Divine at The Woods with co-owner Carl Bruno

CHAPTER THIRTY TWO:
Party at Elfland

An artist named Christo Vladimitov Javacheff and his wife Jeanne-Claude were known for creating enormous temporary outdoor installations. In the early 1970s they built a wall of more than 2,000 panels of white nylon fabric nearly twenty feet tall that followed the contours of the hills across nearly 25 miles of farmland in Marin and Sonoma Counties, ending in the Pacific Ocean. *Christo's Running Fence* stood for fourteen days and then the panels of fabric were given away to the local farmers.

I never saw the fence myself, but I remember a large framed photograph of at least part of the amazing thing. It hung on the wall of a restaurant I liked. People who lived in those parts of the country still talked about Christo and his project years later.

At around the same time as the *Running Fence*, another artist created a place he called Elfland. I heard people talk about him too, how he had been a hippie carpenter who inherited a million dollars, back in the days when a million dollars was a lot of money. He bought a sizeable number of acres of land west of Guerneville with part of the money. It was in a canyon that still had one old building barely standing, a barn that was so weathered you could see right through the spaces between the remaining boards of its walls.

This hippie carpenter did a lot of acid and spent a year or two filling the canyon with creations he made just for the elves he must have hallucinated. He built several sets of elf-sized wooden staircases running up and down the sides of the canyon. They were beautifully made and perfect for a small child. Humans took them two or three steps at a time. He built cement toad stools for the elves to sit on or hide under and two or three little houses, larger than elf-sized but not big enough to be ostentatious.

I heard stories about this crazy hippie riding down the main street of Guerneville in a golden horse-drawn carriage he had built for his bride, if he ever found her. He never found her at the Russian River, I gathered, so he eventually sold Elfland and moved on to live somewhere in the Hawaiian Islands.

I dated a guy for a while who lived in one of the little houses on Elfland. That was how I got to see it for the first time. His bed was in a loft above the kitchen and the ceiling was so low it was hard to have sex up there, not to mention too hot, so we usually did it outside or at my place on Orchard Avenue.

I'll call him Tom because I don't remember his name. It's funny that I remember finding out he was in a lot of porn and his "professional" name was Carl. How do I remember that? This was long before the internet and even before everyone had a DVD player or a Betamax. Gay guys bought their porn in magazines, the way straight guys bought *Hustler* or *Playboy*—glossy, full-color magazines, but the gay ones had fewer articles. Tom/Carl was a popular nude model in those days.

If anyone has any old '70s porn lying around, he had a tattoo of the sun on his chest, just below his left shoulder, and a porn-worthy cock, of course, fat and cut with low-hanging balls. He was also very cute in a nerdy way, especially in real life when he had on his wire-rim glasses. He never wore them in porn.

I don't remember how I met Tom and he didn't last long. I know I said that we "dated," but the truth is that we basically just fucked a few times, maybe went out to breakfast or dinner now and then. He wasn't one of the guys I went with to the ocean or to explore the region. Tom moved back to the city and I never saw him again. I barely thought of him again until now, thinking back to Elfland, but all my memories of him are good ones. I would love to know if he's still alive.

Sometime after Tom moved away, I was invited to a party at Elfland. The invitation was very fancy and engraved with my name on the envelope and a card inside that I was to bring along for entry. The party was on a Saturday night and I had to work until 2 a.m. at The Woods, but as soon as I got cashed out at the end of my shift, I hopped in my truck and headed to Elfland.

At least a hundred cars were lining both sides of the narrow road and dozens of motorcycles, even a few bicycles. I lucked out when someone who had parked near the entrance pulled away. It was a very hot summer night and I could hear the dance music thumping away in the distance. A handsome shirtless man with long flowing hair took my invitation card and said, "Welcome!" I would have been happy to stay right there and get to know him, but more people arrived behind me and he was busy, so I went on ahead.

Tents lined the top of the ridge of the canyon, so I guess the party was going on for longer than just this one night. I don't know how anyone could sleep with that music playing. Maybe the tents were for sex, but there was plenty of that going on outside. I ran into a couple of friends—fuck-buddies, really—who passed

me a joint and showed me where the beer was. We walked down
to the bottom of the canyon where the little elf staircases led to a
cauldron of fruit punch spiked with LSD. That was all I needed!
The stairs were lined with votive candles, so the whole place looked
enchanted under the stars.

We climbed up the other side of the canyon to the old barn,
which someone had wrapped in yards and yards of white fabric
that had once been part of *Christo's Running Fence.* I could see
light coming through the holes in the walls, a light show to rival
any permanent disco in the city and a DJ they'd imported from
somewhere to play great music all night long.

Looking back on that night, it really was magical. We danced
and we drank and we made out with each other in groups of twos
and threes and fours. I guess I always took magical times like those
for granted when I was that age. I don't remember leaving the
party at Elfland. I'm sure I had to be at work at 4 p.m. for T-Dance
on Sunday afternoon. I was probably still flying on acid but I'm
sure my bar back, Earl, and I had plenty of cocaine in case I started
to lag.

CHAPTER THIRTY THREE:
Etta James

Etta James sang at The Woods at least twice a year. The first time I met her I really didn't know her music, but for some reason she really grew to like me. I remember one Monday afternoon in my second or third season at the river, we were setting up the room and getting ready for a sound check when it must have been 100 degrees in the shade. Etta's tour bus pulled up to the front door and her musicians arranged their equipment on and around the stage. Etta came in and saw me from across the room. This was at a time in her life when she was very heavy and on this day she was only wearing sneakers, a pair of skin tight slacks and a bra. She screamed across the room at me, "Baby! Come here and give Etta some lovin'!"

She threw her arms around me and pressed my head into her sweat-soaked breasts until I pleaded for air. "Etta, you know I love you, but I can't breathe! It's too hot for all that right now."

Her shows never started on time. If they were scheduled for 10 o'clock, the audience would all be seated and on their second or third round of drinks before the band members would even start to appear. Maybe it was a good thing that they were drinking and some of them smoking pot too, no doubt. The room was already filled with cigarette smoke, even with all the doors onto the deck wide open. Excitement built until Etta James finally took the stage and rocked the house.

She hated everyone sitting down when she sang. She wanted her audience up and dancing. By the time she was into her second number, people nearest the stage would have pushed their tables and chairs out of the way. When they got up to dance, no one behind them could see, so they stood up too. The cocktail waiters' jobs suddenly became very tricky, trying to keep track of which stoned dancers had been at which tables, running up which bar tabs.

Etta might have gone on singing all night, but the DJ must have taken over eventually and Etta and her band finally left the stage and went back to their rooms. I remember the housekeepers always complained the next day about having to dispose of used hypodermic needles from the rooms where Etta and her band had spent the night. I was shocked the first time I heard that news. I really had no idea. She always seemed to me like she was just having a good time. Years later, I read articles about her kicking the drug habit, losing a lot of weight and looking good. It seemed like she was putting out a new album every year until she died of leukemia in 2012.

In 2008 Beyoncé (billed as Beyoncé Knowles) played Etta James in the film *Cadillac Records* and performed what was perhaps her most famous song, "At last…my love has come along…my lonely days are over…and life is like a song," as well as "Trust in Me," "I'd rather go Blind," "All I Could Do Was Cry," and "Once In A Lifetime."

There are mixed stories about Etta's reaction to the film, but the following year when Beyoncé sang "At Last" for the Obama's first dance at the presidential inauguration, she was quoted as saying, "I'm gonna whup Beyoncé's ass."

These days I hear Etta's voice on television commercials singing "At last" or "Something's got a hold on me" to advertise everything from luxury cars to restaurants to life insurance and I wonder how many people even know who that powerful voice belonged to.

CHAPTER THIRTY FOUR:
Homesick for San Francisco

During Gay Pride weekend in San Francisco, Guerneville feels like a ghost town. It fills up again right afterward with tourists from all over the country and the world and stays crazy busy right through the fourth of July. Then it settles back into the rhythm of the normal busy summer season.

One year on Pride Sunday I was crazy homesick for San Francisco, but I had to work T-Dance at The Woods like always. Business was so slow that they let me close down the patio bar early, so I jumped in my truck and made a beeline to Santa Rosa and risked a speeding ticket all the way down Highway 101 until the Golden Gate Bridge came into view and the traffic forced me to slow down. It was my birthday weekend and I wanted to party!

It was about 5 o'clock in the afternoon and the parade was already finished but I managed to find a parking spot somewhere in the Tenderloin and walk over to the Civic Center. The festival was still going strong, even though the fog was pouring in and cooling things off. Thousands of people were out there in their rainbow-colored everything, but I felt kind of lost and lonely in that crowd. I didn't see anyone I knew and whatever music or speeches that were coming from the main stage were so jumbled and distorted from where I stood that they only sounded like more noise.

I'm not usually one to let things get me down, but I was starting to regret coming down from the river. I hadn't even packed a change of clothes. All I had was the clothes I was wearing and a jacket I always left behind the seat of my truck. I had my cigarettes and a lighter, of course. I soon got tired of the scene at the Civic Center and drove over to the Castro, where I felt a little more like I was "home" but it also made me realize that I didn't really live there fulltime anymore. I stopped in at Castro Station and Toad Hall on Castro Street and the Badlands on 18TH Street, back when it was a real gay bar and restaurant, instead of the cha-cha twinkie palace it became in later years. Those had been my usual stomping grounds in the late '70s, but I didn't run into any of my old friends I used to meet for drinks after work. The bars were all packed with tourists and strangers instead.

I left the Castro and drove down to South of Market to the Ambush. That was more like it. I knew the bartenders there, at least, and ran into a few of the guys I had tricked with at some point in my early 20's. The guy who sold poppers was in his usual corner behind the pool table, so I bought a brown bottle from him for five dollars and decided to head to the baths.

I parked outside the Hothouse, my favorite bathhouse at the time, and found a couple of good-sized roaches in my truck's ashtray. I smoked what was left of both of them and had a much better time from then on.

The next morning when I drove back up to the river on very little sleep, I got to thinking. During my first five years in San Francisco I had made lots of friends, but many of them had moved on. Not all of them, but enough for me to notice the difference. San Francisco had been the siren call for generations of gay men, a place that nearly all of us wanted to experience—the beauty, the freedom, the history, the *men*! But some of us only needed San Francisco for a while, a decade maybe, or only a couple of years. Others are happy with coming to San Francisco for a vacation now and then, or just a weekend once in their lives, just so that they can say that they saw it and hopefully go back to wherever they came from with a happy memory.

The Russian River was only an extension of the San Francisco experience, especially in the summer. I started to realize that by working at the river I had gotten to know more people who were part of San Francisco than I ever had when I lived in the city. I had gotten to be friends with lots of bar people—bar owners and managers and bartenders and disc jockeys and bouncers. I got to know the entertainers who performed at The Woods who lived in San Francisco and Los Angeles, mostly. I had gotten to know people who worked for the newspapers and who were on television. And they got to know me.

I was really having a lot of fun and by the time I was ready to move back to the city, I knew ten times more people than I had before I left. Those years at the river had been an incredible time and I felt part of a large group of great people just before the plague happened.

CHAPTER THIRTY FIVE:

One more winter up north

Toward the end of my second season at The Woods, Jonathan was talking about putting the house on Orchard Avenue up for sale. He had sunk a lot of money into it with the remodel from a single family home into three separate rental units, but he would still make a huge profit by asking twice what he paid for the place. In hindsight, I also wonder whether Jon sensed that he was sick and would only get sicker.

I started looking around for another place to live that fall and ended up making an arrangement with the owners of The Woods to stay there in one of the cabins during the off-season. They gave me cabin #1, just across the footbridge over Fife Creek and the closest one to the main building. During the winter months, they cut back to minimal staff and the three owners spent a lot of time back in Southern California where they came from.

Those of us who stayed through the winter worked under the table for cash and tips. We each went into the unemployment office in Santa Rosa and claimed that we were laid off for the winter so that we could collect benefits. I didn't have to pay any rent for the cabin but instead worked a few hours a week at the front desk answering phones in addition to bartending weekends.

I read a lot of books that winter because the phone rarely rang and when it did, it was easy enough for me to spend a few minutes taking down the caller's credit card number to reserve a room or a cabin. Gay couples found The Woods to be a romantic getaway in the winter, especially if they booked a room with a fireplace or a wood-burning stove.

They told me that some big-name movie stars had stayed in cabin #1 over the years. John Wayne had stayed there when he was making a TV commercial for Great Western somewhere in Sonoma County.

Elizabeth Taylor had spent a night in cabin #1, also back in the day when she would have dined at the elegant Hexagon House restaurant. Nobody could remember which husband she was married to at the time and there was no trace of her White Diamonds perfume after so many years had passed.

Cabin #1 wasn't what I would exactly call romantic for me, but I did have a lot of fun that winter despite sometimes day-long gaps between seeing another human being. I wrote in *For My Brothers* about Patrick Toner, long before he was International Mister Leather, getting flooded in there with me that winter and running around naked searching for firewood one night when the power went out.

On the weekends cabin #1 was very convenient when I got off work at 2 a.m. to invite a bar customer over to spend the night or only as long as it took us to have sex. If that didn't happen, there was always the hot tub. Sometimes on quiet nights during the week I'd be in my cabin watching television or having something to eat when I would see headlights reflected from across the way. I would wait until they parked out by the hot tub and give the guy a few minutes to get naked and relaxed in the steaming soak. Then I would go over there and pretend to be surprised that there was someone there and ask if they minded if I joined them. They never did.

I had a few regular buddies who came by now and then just for sex. Guys in that category were apt to be locals who lived at the river year-round. We didn't want to get too close because as soon as the season started up again in the spring we would all go back to being the whores we were all summer. We were so young!

By spring of that year I knew I had to also move out of cabin #1 so that they could rent it out by the night again to tourists. I asked around and looked at notices on 3x5 cards on the bulletin boards of laundromats and found a little place in Rio Nido to rent for my final summer. It was really just a shack on the side of a steep hill on a crooked street called Rotunda Way. The place was so small the refrigerator had to go outside on the tiny deck beside the water heater.

I had no heat but a wood burning stove. The kitchen stove took gas, but I had to change the tank myself every few weeks and take the empty one into Guerneville to get it refilled. My bed took up most of the main room and the tiny kitchen and bathroom were, to be generous, "utilitarian" in size. There were no stairs or sidewalks. I just had to climb up a steep and often muddy hill from where I parked my truck below. There was no mail service, so I just had my parents send me their letters at The Woods.

The place was so cheap I didn't much mind all that it lacked. It was mine. One of my few belongings in those days was a big, bulky television set I had bought at a thrift store in San Francisco. It was so old it had tubes inside and it weighed a ton. One day I came home to find a cardboard flyer on my doorknob. Someone had actually climbed up there to let me know that I could get cable television. The reception under the Rio Nido redwood trees was pretty iffy with just rabbit ears.

The next time I saw my bar back Earl at work I mentioned it to him. He and his boyfriend David lived in a house—not a shack like mine—up the hill from me, just across the street and around the corner. Earl told me David hooked up their cable and he could do mine too, so not to pay for it. The next day David came over with a ladder and climbed up a tall pole and voila, I had free cable TV.

Now I had twelve channels. No cable box. No remote control. No problem. Twelve channels were more than enough for me. I wasn't home that much and didn't watch TV very often unless I was bored and I rarely had time to be bored.

About a week later my cable stopped working one morning. I looked out the window and saw a yellow truck parked outside with a guy in a hard hat in a cherry picker bucket up on the pole. I noticed later that he had already left another cardboard flyer on my doorknob and wondered how he had done that without my hearing him, but I might have been in the shower. This time the flyer highlighted the number to call to order cable installation.

Earl's boyfriend David must have seen the truck too because as soon as it drove away he brought back out his ladder and hooked my cable up again. It worked from then on for as long as I lived in Rio Nido. It never occurred to me at the time that my parents would have been ashamed of me for stealing something that other people paid for. I was just grateful to have such a thoughtful neighbor.

When I finally moved back to San Francisco and rented an apartment in the South of Market area, I couldn't get cable TV. My block wasn't residential enough. I was amazed that I get it for free in a falling down shack on the side of a hill in that little canyon under the redwoods, but it still wasn't available in certain parts of the city.

One of the best things about living in Rio Nido was a hidden little road that was a shortcut from deep in the canyon leading out to Armstrong Woods Road. It was barely more than one lane for most of the way but I rarely met another vehicle on it. Parts of it weren't even paved. I could drive to work at The Woods without having to go through Guerneville at all. Better yet, I could take it home after work without risking getting stopped by the cops on River Road. They were notorious for stopping drivers and giving breathalyzers, especially on weekends after the bars closed.

Someday I'd like to drive up to Rio Nido again, turn to the right of the Rio Nido Lodge where folks used to dance to the big band sounds of Glen Miller and Tommy Dorsey or listen to singers like Frank Sinatra and Helen Forest on those lazy, long ago nights along the Russian River. I'll drive a little deeper into the darkness of the towering trees up Canyon 2 Road to look for Rotunda Way and see if that little shack is still perched on the side of the hill.

CHAPTER THIRTY SIX:
Gay Cancer

During the summers that I lived at the Russian River I didn't drive down to San Francisco nearly as often as I did in the wintertime. Sonoma County was too beautiful to want to leave it very often and it seemed like all the men I could ever want were coming to me from all over the world.

I had to drive down now and then, of course, to see old friends I knew from my first five years in San Francisco and the many new friends I had made because they came up to The Woods on weekends. I always had a choice of places to stay in the city and most trips included at least one night at the baths. My earliest favorite, the Folsom Street Barracks, burned down in July of 1981 and another one I loved, the Fair Oaks Hotel on the corner of Oak and Steiner in the Western Addition, had already closed down in 1979. The Ritch Street Baths were still going strong, though. That was where Sylvester sometimes held court in their enormous Jacuzzi and where I sometimes saw Rudolph Nureyev when he was in town. I could have been the one who gave him AIDS but we knew nothing about that at the time.

The 21st Street Baths in the Mission district still had a great blue-collar, workingman's kind of vibe but Ritch Street seemed too tame for me after I discovered places like The Slot, The Hothouse, and The Handball Express, which was upstairs and next door to The End-Up at 6ᵀᴴ and Harrison.

I usually stayed with my friend Roger when I came down to the city from the Russian River. He lived on Seward Street, which was convenient for eating, shopping, daytime drinking, and of course cruising in the Castro. I just happened to be out there one day in 1981 when I saw a group of guys my age standing outside Star Pharmacy at 498 Castro Street at the corner of 18ᵀᴴ Street. Everyone was staring at a sign in the window that said "GAY CANCER" across the top and had pictures taped to it that showed someone's body with dark lesions speckled across the skin.

There exists a famous photograph by Rink, a well-known San Francisco photographer, of a group of men standing in that spot, looking at that poster. I am not in that photograph, but I might have been standing there a few minutes earlier or later. What I remember about being there in that moment was how quiet we all were. No one spoke. We just read what was on the sign and stared at the pictures, the first visual evidence I ever saw that depicted what was coming.

I found out later that Bobbi Campbell was the person who had posted the sign. The pictures were of his own lesions. I knew Bobbi from before I moved up to the river. He was a registered nurse and one of the original Sisters of Perpetual Indulgence, known as Sister Florence Nightmare. He would later appear on the cover of *Newsweek* and become known across the country as the "AIDS poster boy." Bobbi had Kaposi's sarcoma, an opportunistic disease that causes painless purple lesions. It was so rare that it was only known in parts of Africa and the Mediterranean, up until the early 1980s.

Even now, nearly forty years later, writing about that moment when I stared at that sign, surrounded by young men I didn't know, guys just like me, I wince a little and want to clutch my chest, not literally, but… I want to go back to that day and hug each one of those guys on Castro Street in front of Star Pharmacy. I want to encourage them in their long climb up Mount Everest that we were all about to attempt together. I wish I could go back and see all of their young lives' future joys and successes in the newspapers instead of most of their obituaries.

I drove back up north to the river the next day and tried not to think too much about that sign in the window on 18TH and Castro. Guerneville was an hour and a half from the city and it seemed like we were still several months removed from having to face this strange new disease. We even made morbid jokes about it:

Q—"What's the hardest part about getting Gay Cancer?"

A—"Convincing your parents that you're Haitian."

I remember one evening at the Rainbow Cattle Company on Guerneville's Main Street, talking with friends about this new gay disease. On Sunday nights after I was finished working T-Dance at The Woods, I usually went to the Rainbow with a group of friends. They had a game where lucky winners got a chance to spin a wheel for prizes of free drink tickets and t-shirts and such things. Most of the gay resorts had bars in them, but when I wanted to feel like I was in a "real" bar, like the bars in the city, the RBCC was the closest thing. I liked to play pool there too. I was never very good at it, but we played constantly, especially when things slowed down on the weeknights or off-season.

Someone mentioned gay cancer and it turned out nearly everyone had heard some gossip they wanted to share. Someone had heard that you could get it from one of the ingredients in a certain brand of deodorant—not the spray or the roll-on kind, they said—only the stick version.

Someone else had heard that you could get it from poppers, especially the big name-brands like Rush and Bolt and Hardware. He heard it was a government plot to kill off all the gays. The only safe poppers were locally made. I had always bought mine from the "popper guy" who hung out south of Market and could usually be found at the Ambush. They came in a plain brown bottle with no label at all. Five bucks. They were strong too, and didn't have the sweet, perfumed smell of some of the mass-produced names.

I heard on the news one day that a huge fire broke out in a building near the SOMA waterfront and the smoke was so thick it enveloped part of the western end of the Bay Bridge. The next day we heard it was a popper factory that had blown up. We all laughed about those drivers on the bridge getting a big hit of poppers and losing control of their vehicles, smashing into each other on their way into or out of San Francisco.

We worried that we might not be able to get any more of our favorite poppers after that, but the next time I went to the Ambush the popper guy was there. Five bucks. No problem. I was so relieved!

Back to that night at the Rainbow...we talked about the possibility of some kind of poison in the water supply, but just in certain neighborhoods like the Castro and only in specific cities like New York and San Francisco and maybe Los Angeles. But then wouldn't straight people get it too? Maybe they did, but we just hadn't heard about them yet. There was a lot of confusion in those early days.

Maybe it was in a certain brand of beer that they only sold in gay bars. Or maybe it was on the bar glasses. Or the soap they washed them in? Or the disinfectant? I knew some guys who started drinking through a straw so their lips wouldn't touch the rim of the glass. Most of the glasses we used at The Woods were plastic and disposable, especially around the pools and in the disco. Some guys switched from drinking mixed drinks to drinking strictly beer—imported beer, to be on the safe side.

Other than that night at the Rainbow Cattle Company, I don't remember many conversations about gay cancer in those very early days. Cases were few and far between. It was only happening to people we didn't know (aside from Bobbi Campbell) in big cities. We were still at a safe distance up at the river.

We never even considered, living in a resort town, that people from the big cities were coming to us all summer long and on holidays and weekends the rest of the year. We never even considered at first that this strange new scary disease that was gradually creeping into all of our thoughts, no matter how subconsciously, could possibly have anything to do with sex.

We gay men were an army of lovers. Nothing could change that. Sex was a huge part of our lives, especially in our 20s and 30s. We may have recently lost Harvey Milk, but our freedoms were only going to grow. Everything we saw in society was moving in the right direction. Openly gay people were actually being depicted on television sitcoms, usually as comic foils, but at least we were there, unlike during my childhood. There would be plenty of time to slow down when we got older, maybe fall in love, maybe settle down with one (or two) special partners, trade in our lives on the dance floor for a nice big kitchen, maybe a fireplace, and even a deck with a view.

Ever so slowly we heard about people getting sick who were friends of friends, but sometimes it would turn out to be just regular pneumonia—thank God, not gay pneumonia! A few people started to die from "opportunistic infections," whatever they were, but no one I knew very well, not at first, anyway.

One day I was home alone when the telephone rang and it was Mister Marcus, who wrote the leather column for the weekly B.A.R. newspaper in San Francisco. He had recently been up to

The Woods to MC one of the contests I had organized. He was calling to tell me that one of the contestants—I'll call him Jay—was found dead in the steam room of the 21st Street Baths.

Jay was a bartender at Badlands on 18ᵀᴴ Street in the Castro, back when Badlands had a restaurant in the back, instead of the dance floor they have now. Jay was a great guy, sexy, friendly, and very popular. He hadn't won that contest at The Woods—I think he came in second or third—and had spent a night with me on Orchard Avenue after the contest was over. I never slept with contestants until afterward, so no one could accuse me of fixing things.

It seemed strange to me that Jay would have gone to the baths if he was that sick, but we later found out that he had shot up speed right before he went into the steam room where he died of a massive heart attack. I was shocked! I was no prude, but I hadn't thought I knew anyone who did needle drugs. That was hardcore! Still, I spoke the words I would say dozens of times again in the months and years to come, over the phone that day with Marcus, "Well, at least it wasn't gay cancer."

By the autumn of my third full year at the Russian River, I started to hear about people dying of AIDS. We were calling it AIDS by then, I think. People I had known as customers or friends' ex-lovers or next-door neighbors of old boyfriends of mine. There was some talk of The Woods being sold and I decided that I didn't want to go through the upheaval of finding a different job at the river or finding the lay of the land with new owners running the place. As things worked out, no sale went through that year. I could have stayed for another season, but something told me it was time for me to move on, which meant to move back "home" to San Francisco.

In my three years away from the city, I had gotten to know far more people who lived there than I had in my early twenties while I was waiting tables and going to graduate school at SFSU. Bartending, maître d'-ing, and producing contests and special events at The Woods had allowed me to meet dozens of San Francisco bar owners and bar patrons, not to mention entertainers from all over the country, and become friends with many of them. If any of them got sick, maybe I could be there to help them and besides, I didn't want to go through one more winter of rain and floodwaters rising.

I thought about those guys outside of Star Pharmacy that afternoon, how quiet we were as we looked at those pictures of Bobbi Campbell's lesions, how numbed I felt about staring into what might be my future. I felt connected to those other young men, somehow, even though we were strangers, silent in the face of illness and death, while even the sounds of cars and buses and taxicabs and fire trucks seemed to fade away and leave us in that moment of silence and dread.

If my people were going to start going through something scary, I wanted to be there with them. I thought back to the day when Harvey Milk was shot and killed, how thousands of us carried candles that night from the Castro to City Hall in a daze of grief. We couldn't have envisioned how AIDS would change our world, but we could at least be together. I wanted to be there with my friends, my brothers, in San Francisco, while we tried to envision what was coming at us and figure out what to do next.

THIRTY SEVEN:
Afterword—One Last Hurrah with Eartha Kitt

I moved back to San Francisco during the winter of 1983-'84. Jim Cvitanich had recently won the title of Mister San Francisco Leather and asked me to help him co-produce *Men Behind Bars—the bartenders' folly* on a Monday night in January at the Victoria Theater. It was one of the first big fundraisers to fight AIDS and would become an annual event that took up most of my spare time for about the next decade.

That spring I got a call from one of the owners of The Woods telling me that they needed me to come back in the spring to produce the Mr. Northern California Drummer contest one more time. They had already negotiated with *Drummer* magazine to put the dates on the calendar and booked entertainment for Saturday night in the disco, but they needed someone to get the contestants and sponsors and judges lined up and coordinate the advertising. In a way, it was just as easy for me to do most of that from the city as it was at the river.

The big disco act they had booked was a Canadian husband and wife duo called Lime, which I had never even heard of. When I looked them up on YouTube while writing this book I discovered that their song "Babe We're Gonna Love Tonight" is one I probably danced to a thousand times in the '80s, but I never knew the name of the group who did it.

I got posters made and put them up in every gay bar in San Francisco, bought a two-page center spread ad in the *Bay Area Reporter*, and then Carl Bruno called me from The Woods to let me know that Lime canceled, but he had already booked Earth Kitt instead for Saturday night on the dance floor.

I was beyond thrilled! Eartha Kitt, with her sultry voice and sexy attitude, had taken over the role Catwoman from Julie Newmar on the old TV show *Batman*. She had been in movies and I had once seen her cabaret act at the old Mocambo nightclub on Polk Street. So I went back out to hit the streets with a felt tip pen and a sheet of white stickers and covered over Lime on the posters in every bar in San Francisco.

Eartha Kitt had released a disco single called "Where is My Man?" so I knew she would be doing that number but I didn't know what else to expect. When the weekend came, I spent some time with all the contestants after their Saturday afternoon interviews out beside the nude pool, rehearsing carrying a velvet-covered platform which would bear Miss Kitt high above their heads and across the dance floor like Elizabeth Taylor in *Cleopatra* and then lower her gently to the stage at midnight.

We knew that Eartha Kitt was performing earlier that same night at Davies Symphony Hall in San Francisco, so we arranged for a limousine to pick her up there and drive her to the Russian River. There was plenty of time for her to arrive by midnight. I found out later that nobody bothered to tell her that the ride would take about an hour and a half. She thought she was just going to another venue across town to perform. She must have gotten a little suspicious when the driver crossed the Golden Gate Bridge and kept going north.

It was just past eleven when someone found me to let me know that her limo had just pulled up outside, so I ran out to greet her, show her to her dressing room, and explain about the eight half-naked muscular young men who would carry her to the stage. She got a crazed look in her eyes and said to me, "*Oh, no!* I'm going on *now* or I'm not going on at all!"

I said, "Just give a minute to let the DJ know what's happening." I ran inside, cued the sound and light guys, got her microphone onstage, and grabbed a few of the beefiest guys around me to form a human wall from the edge of the stage to the side door where she would enter. There was no way to get those eight guys in place in such a short time. I ran back outside and Eartha Kitt took my arm to lead her inside and up the steps onto the stage.

The crowd went wild for her, of course. They weren't dancing so much as they were pressed up against the stage on all sides and whistling from the balconies all the way around that hexagonal room where everyone from Betty Hutton and Sharon McNight to Divine and Morgana King had once performed. They were all cheering and clapping with their arms in the air.

The next thing I knew, she was reaching for me to help her back down the stairs and out to the limousine. She said to me, "You guys are too much!"

I said, "So are you, Miss Kitt, so are you!" which she took as a compliment as she sat down and the chauffer closed the door and whisked her back to SFO for a flight to somewhere in Germany for her next engagement.

The next day, beside the swimming pools at The Woods, people said what a great time they were having and congratulated me on the contest and told me how thrilled they were to have seen Eartha Kitt in person. Maybe they had all been so stoned the night before that nobody noticed that she was only on stage for about five minutes. Most of the contestants missed her act entirely because they were getting ready to put on their matching black Speedos at midnight.

Drummer Poster

On Sunday afternoon Sonny Cline was declared the winner of the Mister Northern California Drummer contest and would go on to win the title of International Mister Drummer. I tracked him down through Facebook and discovered that he now lives in New Jersey. I asked him what he remembered about that contest and he said, "Yes, I remember I'm not that old yet. LOL. 1984. It was a hot and sweaty balls-dripping night."

I spent one more night at The Woods and woke up late on Monday, packed my bags and drove back down to San Francisco. I didn't return to the Russian River, even for a visit, for many years. I was tending bar on Castro Street one day when I heard the news that the main hexagonal building at The Woods had burned to the ground. I almost shed a tear before I told myself to just be grateful for a lot of wonderful memories.

Guerneville, here we come!

The "shack" on Rotunda Way

The infamous Room #20

The Rainbow Cattle Company

I finally DID take a trip up to the Russian River after I finished writing this book. The old shack on the side of a hill in Rio Nido is still there, but it looks like new with beautiful redwood decks and stairs where there was only a muddy hillside before. The Hexagonal building that once housed an art school, an elegant restaurant, and finally a fabulous dance floor, is long gone, but I ignored the No Trespassing signs and got to see the old *Flintstones* pool, neglected and full of leaves now. At least I got to take a picture of room 20, where all of the celebrities stayed and we watched Divine eat chocolate cake in *flagrante delicto*. The big blue house on Orchard Avenue has been replaced by an even bigger house behind a tall wooden fence, but the Russian River is as beautiful as ever, still winding its way to Jenner-by-the-Sea.

*Index of Recognizable Names
sorted by first name or familiar term
Showing major appearance*

About the Author

Mark Abramson is the author of the *Beach Reading* mystery series, set in San Francisco's gay Castro district, as well as six non-fiction diaries and memoirs, including this one. He worked as a bartender and event planner for many years and now devotes most of his time to writing. He can be contacted through his website: http://www.markabramson.net

Praise for:

Minnesota Boy
"It's not quite a follow up book to his much needed and well-written memoir *For My Brothers*, but it is a terrific read and what makes it so readable is that Abramson isn't out to show how differently fabulous he is, but how ordinarily wonderful. His tale… is both all-American and way-out-there."
—Felice Picano, author of *The Lure* and *Justify My Sins*

*Sex, Drugs & Disco – San Francisco Diaries
from the Pre-AIDS Era*
"Reporting live from the wild 1970s party in the Castro, Mark Abramson outs the daily diary he wrote forty years ago, on location in real time, in this rowdy and thrilling eyewitness memoir. Authentic as Walt Whitman's sex diaries, his past is our past. Miss the 1970s? Born too late? Curl up with this author of a good book."
—Jack Fritscher, author of *Some Dance to Remember:
A Memoir-Novel of San Francisco 1970 – 1982*

The BEACH READING series
"Part of the appeal of the series is that Abramson sticks to the reality of San Francisco—the Castro, in particular. He writes what he knows, drawing on his experiences in the community as a waiter-bartender. Local readers can recognize the stores and bars they frequent; Abramson even features a few San Francisco celebs in cameos.

"The idea is to draw readers into a world they know. The series is both familiar and escapist. It's aggressively unpretentious, because that's the kind of book Abramson wants to read."
—Louis Peitzman, *San Francisco Chronicle*

Printed in Great Britain
by Amazon

37900111R00128